Fanciful Paper Flowers

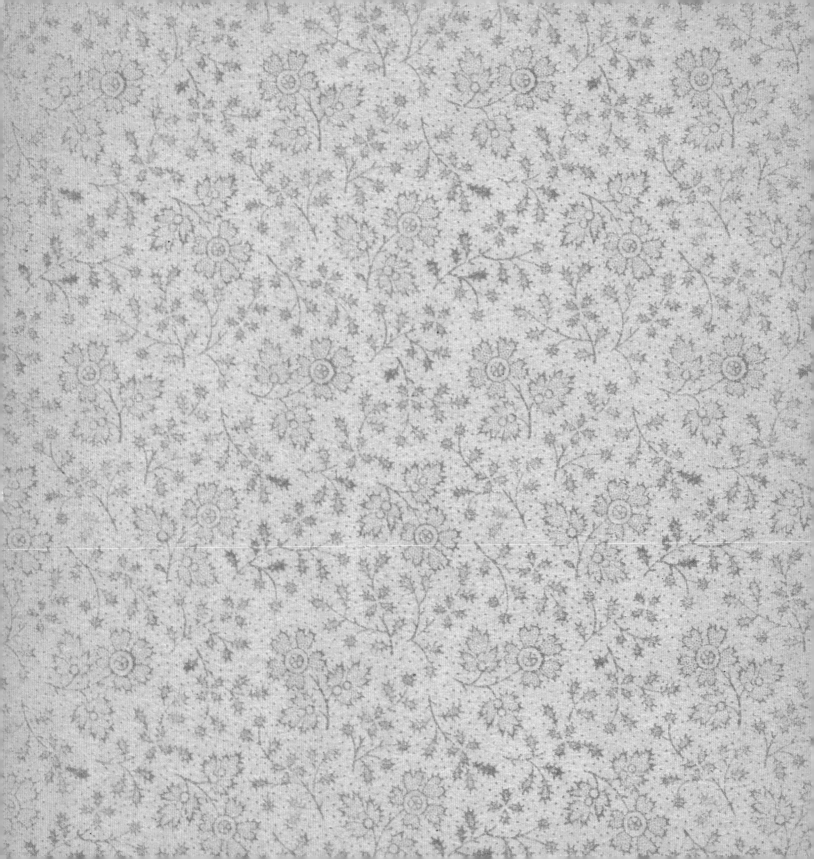

Fanciful Paper Flowers:
Creative Techniques
for Crafting an Enchanted Garden

Sandra Evertson

A LARK/CHAPELLE BOOK

A Division of Sterling Publishing Co., Inc.
New York

EDITOR
Kathy Sheldon

ASSISTANT EDITOR
Julie Hale

EDITORIAL ASSISTANCE
Delores Gosnell

ART DIRECTOR
Susan McBride

PHOTOGRAPHY
Thomas McConnell

COVER DESIGN
Thom Gaines

ASSOCIATE ART DIRECTOR
Shannon Yokeley

PRODUCTION ASSISTANT
Jeff Hamilton

ART INTERNS
Courtney Tiberio
Amelia Hancock

A Lark/Chapelle Book

Chapelle, Ltd., Inc.
P.O. Box 9255, Ogden, UT 84409
(801) 621-2777 • (801) 621-2788 Fax
e-mail: chapelle@chapelleltd.com
Web site: www.chapelleltd.com

Library of Congress Cataloging-in-Publication Data

Evertson, Sandra.
  Fanciful paper flowers : creative techniques for crafting an enchanted
garden / Sandra Evertson. -- 1st ed.
      p. cm.
  Includes index.
  ISBN 1-60059-027-6 (pbk.)
  1. Paper flowers. I. Title.
  TT892.E94 2007
  745.594'3--dc22

                                    2006028356

10 9 8 7 6 5 4 3 2 1

First Edition

Published by Lark Books, A Division of
Sterling Publishing Co., Inc.
387 Park Avenue South, New York, N.Y. 10016

Text © 2007, Sandra Evertson
Photography © 2007, Lark Books
Illustrations © 2007, Lark Books

Distributed in Canada by Sterling Publishing,
c/o Canadian Manda Group, 165 Dufferin Street
Toronto, Ontario, Canada M6K 3H6

Distributed in the United Kingdom by GMC Distribution Services,
Castle Place, 166 High Street, Lewes, East Sussex, England BN7 1XU

Distributed in Australia by Capricorn Link (Australia) Pty Ltd.,
P.O. Box 704, Windsor, NSW 2756 Australia

Manufactured in China
All rights reserved
ISBN 13: 978-1-60059-027-6
ISBN 10: 1-60059-027-6
For information about custom editions, special sales, premium and
corporate purchases, please contact Sterling Special Sales Department at 800-805-5489
or specialsales@sterlingpub.com.

Contents

Introduction

The earth laughs in flowers —Ralph Waldo Emerson

And so will you, once you begin creating these mirthful paper bouquets. Throw away any previous concepts of ordinary, lifeless, and dull botanicals. Prepare yourself for a whole new adventure in flower making. My goal in this book is to inspire a sense of joy in you as you learn to create your own garden of paper fantasy flowers—one that will include everything from hanging tissue posies and postcard florets on winding vines to dipped wax blooms.

I've been crafting for as long as I can remember. I'm always dreaming up new ways of making things. Long intrigued by antique designs, I love those beautiful old millinery flowers tucked in the big Victorian hats of the past and the lovely, colorful, plump velvet and silk rosettes pinned to the hip of a 1920s party dress. I fancy the notion of sophisticated whimsy, bringing a blend of humor and elegance into my work that I'm excited to share with you.

I'm also a lifelong collector of antique ephemera and textiles. When I came across an intriguing old book on paper flowers that had pages full of curled crepe-paper petals, twisted newsprint stems, and folding techniques, I just had to design my own array of paper posies.

This book gives you a peek into my studio to see how that design process unfolded. Each of the ten project chapters features a page from my sketchbook where you'll see the idea in development. I'll then teach the techniques (some new, some exciting twists on the tried-and-true) by giving you step-by-step instructions for three

projects you can make using that technique. The projects are visually stimulating yet easy to do. The designs use common, readily available materials and tools: scissors, paper towel tubes, old newspapers, beeswax, and hole and flower punches. The most important element, fanciful papers, is included. I've provided you with your own virtual flea market of vintage papers to color copy and use.

Once you start on these projects, you'll be amazed by how versatile a medium paper is. Just about anything your mind can dream up can be fashioned out of paper. The first time you turn a flat sheet of paper into a dimensional blossom, you'll feel a fantastic sense of accomplishment. You'll be eager to give your charming paper blossoms away as gifts, add them to your home, and use them to decorate parties and special events.

I love the old Grimm's fairy tales—trees that talk and flowers that sing ignite my imagination. I delight in those mischievous little characters that always seem to turn the fates of the inhabitants in those stories. In turn, I would take great delight in the thought that this book could alter your thinking about paper flowers. I'm very happy to bring my art to you. My wish is to draw you in and tempt you to create. I believe the seed of an artist lies dormant inside each and every one of us; jump in and let these pages help your imagination bloom!

Paper Flower Basics

First word: Toss all preconceived ideas of paper flowers out the window! The fanciful florals in these pages are intricately designed but easy and fun to make. Jump in and have a good time.

Materials & Tools

You don't need any special materials or tools to cultivate these flowers—just the basic supplies any crafter is likely to have around the house. This is a general list; each project also specifies the tools and materials needed.

Paper

I like to use recycled materials such as **paper grocery bags** and **paper towel tubes**. I use recycled copy paper because it's better for the environment and because I find it easier to manipulate. It also seems to take the ink from the photocopier better. Many of the flowers call for **colored cardstock**; I find medium to heavy weight works well.

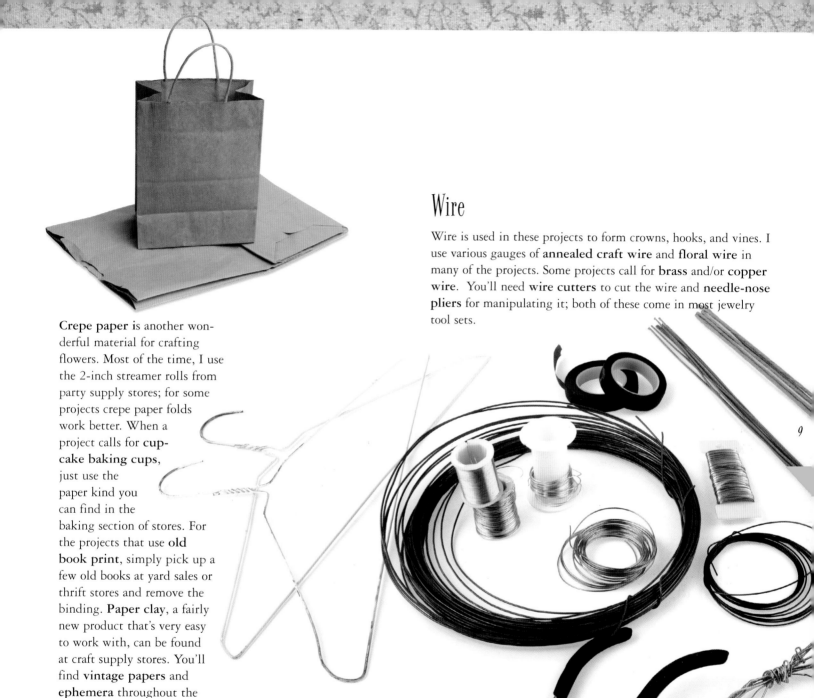

Crepe paper is another wonderful material for crafting flowers. Most of the time, I use the 2-inch streamer rolls from party supply stores; for some projects crepe paper folds work better. When a project calls for **cupcake baking cups,** just use the paper kind you can find in the baking section of stores. For the projects that use **old book print**, simply pick up a few old books at yard sales or thrift stores and remove the binding. **Paper clay**, a fairly new product that's very easy to work with, can be found at craft supply stores. You'll find **vintage papers** and **ephemera** throughout the book to color copy and use in the projects. If you'd like to gather your own papers, see the sidebar Finding Paper Ephemera on page 12.

Wire

Wire is used in these projects to form crowns, hooks, and vines. I use various gauges of **annealed craft wire** and **floral wire** in many of the projects. Some projects call for **brass** and/or **copper wire**. You'll need **wire cutters** to cut the wire and **needle-nose pliers** for manipulating it; both of these come in most jewelry tool sets.

Embellishments

Collect any embellishments that suit your fancy; you never know when you'll find a use for something. Check out the bargain **ribbon** bin at your local craft store and stock up! I collect **beads**, **buttons**, and **costume jewelry** from everywhere, but tag sales are a good source for inexpensive and unusual finds. When it comes to **glitter**, I prefer the appearance of the finely ground ones. Various pastel shades of **glitter glue** will come in handy as well.

Adhesives

I use **carpenter's glue** because it's thicker, stronger, and tackier than white glue, but **white glue** can also be used on many of the projects. When **hot glue** is called for, I prefer a mini hot-glue gun since these smaller ones release less glue and are not as messy as the large ones. **Decoupage medium** (available at craft supply stores) is also used in some projects. Lightly spraying your photocopied images with a **commercial paper spray sealer** will help preserve the paper and prevent colors from fading.

Miscellaneous Items

Toothpicks are perfect for applying the smallest amounts of glue and for rolling up paper to make it curl. You'll need a **needle and thread** in some projects to make gathering stitches and a **pencil** to copy patterns and mark measurements. **Wax paper** works well for smoothing out wrinkles and bubbles on decoupaged pieces, and it also can serve as an easy-clean-up work surface. Other miscellaneous items used in the projects include **polymer clay**, **canning wax**, **clothespins**, and **straight pins**.

Paint

I recommend using **acrylic paints**. My studio is filled with various brands in a rainbow of colors. I found that **disposable sponge brushes** work better than bristle brushes, as they leave no brush marks and make for quick and easy clean-ups. **Cosmetic sponge wedges** work well, too, for certain applications; you can cut and trim a sponge wedge to the appropriate size to get into tight corners or edges.

Access to a Color Photocopier

Because these handy machines are now so much less expensive than they used to be, many crafters own a **color photocopier**. If you do, you'll be able to make color copies of the papers and ephemera I've provided for you in these pages. You can also reproduce family photos, cards, and other mementos. If you don't own a color copier, simply visit your local copy shop.

Cutting Tools

It's nice to have an assortment of **scissors** on hand when you're doing any kind of paperwork. Along with regular **paper scissors**, I like to use **decorative-edge scissors** and small, **curved-bladed scissors** made for fine cutwork. I use ½-inch **circle punches** and ¼- and ⅛-inch **hole punches** in many of these projects. (I'm usually using them to make dots, not holes!) A **flower punch** (available in an assortment of styles at craft supply stores) allows you to make many, many identical flower shapes in minutes.

Sculpting Tools

A package of **plastic clay-sculpting tools** will come in handy for sculpting cardstock petals. The bulbous-tipped tools work well for molding curved forms. Other good items to have on hand as sculpting tools include: **1-inch and 3⅜-inch wooden shaker pegs**, the blunt end of an **old butter knife** (for curling up the edges of a crepe paper floret), and a **2-inch wooden craft egg** (it curls paper bag petals under nicely). Look around your own home and experiment—you never know what you can use as a tool.

FINDING PAPER EPHEMERA

I've included decorative papers and antique images for you to color copy and use when making the flowers. To customize your pieces, you can also use your own ephemera (theatre tickets, birth announcements, family photos, old high school diplomas, wedding invitations, greeting cards—the choices are endless). Spend a nice afternoon reminiscing with an older relative, and go through old family photos, postcards, and correspondence. You can make color copies of cherished family mementos and use those copies to create heirloom flowers your loved ones will appreciate.

Other good sources for antique ephemera are thrift stores, estate sales, and tag sales. Co-op antique malls are especially great for old books, playing cards, and vintage papers, as they feature many little shops within one. My favorite place to search for treasures is still a good old-fashioned outdoor flea market; you never know what riches you'll uncover there.

Tips & Tricks of the Trade

Stop & Look

Before you start each project, sit back and study the photo of the piece for a moment. Train your eye to notice every little detail. This will help you get a good feel for what's involved in making the project. Be sure to refer back to the photo as you work.

Repeat Yourself

Generally, the instructions given are for a single flower. Simply repeat them to make several flowers for lively, lush bouquets.

Wrinkle Cure

Don't concern yourself too much with bubbles and wrinkles when using decoupage medium—they tend to flatten out as the medium dries and stretches the paper. If you do need to smooth a surface, use a folded square of wax paper to gently rub from the center outwards.

Displaying Your Flowers

This book offers many fresh ideas for displaying your new works of art, but don't stop here—let your imagination loose and find unusual ways to display your paper bouquets. Drape a garland of paper posies above a wall mirror, or tie roses to chair backs or bedposts. While hunting for out-of-the-ordinary ephemera, keep an eye out for unique containers. Paint an old rusty bedspring a bright citrus color to make a charming flower vase. Decoupage a dented tin paint can with newsprint and vintage postcards for an amusing container to hold wax-dipped blooms. These flowers aren't conventional—why use ordinary vases? Keep an open mind while shopping, and you'll discover all sorts of common items just waiting to be reborn as works of art!

Last word:

There are no mistakes—just jump in and have fun!

Technique 1:

Flower Punches

We will start out with fun and easy flower punches. This technique is the most basic of all: just slide in a piece of paper, press down, and create hundreds of identical little flowers.

A page from my sketchbook

mint green cardstock

old Book print

[silk covered floral wire

↓ flower punch

Glitter Kitten Crown

green glitter

Glitter Kitten Crown

Celebrate in style! This crown would be darling on any princess or cherub you happen to know, whether she's two or 72. Commemorate a special birthday or other event with this charming keepsake.

What You Need

19-gauge craft wire

Wire cutters

Needle-nose pliers

Old book print

Decoupage medium

Pencil

Flower punch

Mint green cardstock

Brown paper bags

Mint green glitter

Green silk-covered floral wire

Carpenter's glue

Wax paper

The text photo shows a book crown with flowers.

untry. Somehow (and it would be _a_, and who declares ough
rned that th _S..._ ere up. That _oved._[2] Here, as elsev ust
Bridger's absen _er_ maybe the Sioux had _..dical_ passion could _..._ and
plenty of them in his time.) Furthermore, Hastings and F

16

What You Do

1 Unravel approximately 20 inches of the 19-gauge craft wire (you can make this longer or shorter, depending on the desired size of your finished crown). Bend little curlicue loops—some facing up, some facing down—all along the length of the wire (Fig. A).

Fig. A

2 Curl the entire piece into a circle and twist the ends closed.

3 Tear old book print into small ½-inch pieces. Decoupage pieces onto the front side of the wire, then onto the back side of the wire, sandwiching the wire in between and covering right over the curlicue loops.

4 Cover the entire piece, then use a pencil to poke through the loops to make holes. Set aside to dry.

5 Punch out about 25 flowers from the mint green cardstock and about 25 flowers from a brown paper bag. Use scissors to cut 25 little leaf shapes from a brown paper bag (Fig. B).

Fig. B

6 Coat the mint green flowers with a thin layer of decoupage medium, sprinkle with mint green glitter, and let dry.

7 Wind green-silk-covered floral wire loosely around the crown (the way a vine would grow), pinching little bits of it together here and there to look like thorns (Fig. C).

Fig. C

8 Glue the green glitter flowers and the brown bag flowers randomly onto the crown, adding as many or as few as you like—after all, it's your crown! Add in a few brown leaves here and there.

9 To make each flower center, squeeze a dot of carpenter's glue into the palm of your hand and roll it into a tiny ball, then set it aside to dry on a bit of wax paper. Glue each to the center of a flower. Once it's completely dry, place the crown on your head, and begin your reign.

Lavender Hullabaloos

Picture several of these ethereal, butter-yellow orbs hung at varying levels from a beautiful old candelabra. No matter where you put them, they'll create a dreamy, whimsical effect.

WHAT YOU NEED

Yellow crepe paper streamers

Carpenter's glue

2½-inch polystyrene foam balls

Scissors

Flower punch

Cardstock in purple, lavender, and orchid

Small costume pearls

Straight pins

19-gauge craft wire

Needle-nose pliers

Wire cutters

Yellow glass beads

Rhinestone bead dividers

Wire cutters

*The greatest
joys I ever
knew were
those that
came from
meeting you.*

18

What You Do

1 Unravel a couple of feet of the yellow crepe paper streamer, leaving it attached to the roll. Fold the unraveled section of streamer in half horizontally.

2 Put a dab of glue on the top of the polystyrene foam ball. Start winding the crepe paper around the ball, giving the paper a twist at the bottom and again at the top of the ball.

3 Continue around the ball until it's completely covered. Cut off the crepe paper, and use a dab of glue to secure the end.

4 Use the flower punch to cut a variety of florets out of all three colors of cardstock. Place two florets together for each flower, mixing colors.

5 Thread a costume pearl onto a straight pin before stabbing the pin through both florets. Turn each layer so you can see both petal colors. Add a dab of glue to the end of the pin, and poke it into the ball. Place as many or as few florets as you like.

6 To begin making a hanging hook, use the needle-nose pliers to bend a 1-inch piece of the craft wire into the shape of a shepherd's cane (Fig. A).

7 Put a dab of glue just below the cane's crook, then slide on a costume pearl, a yellow glass bead, and two florets. Poke a hole with a straight pin to pierce the crepe paper, add another dab of glue to the end of the wire, and push it into the top of the ball.

8 To make a decorative S hook, cut a 2½-inch piece of craft wire, and bend it at the top into the same shepherd's cane shape. Add a dab of glue just below the crook area, slide on a yellow glass bead, a rhinestone bead divider, and another yellow glass bead, and then bend the end of the wire into another shepherd's cane, facing the opposite direction (Fig. B).

Fig. A

Fig. B

Giggles and Daisies

These tiny white daisies remind me of long summer days idled away on a beautiful green lawn sprinkled with countless numbers of the sweet little blossoms.

WHAT YOU NEED

22-gauge green floral wire

Wire cutters

Needle-nose pliers

Flower punch

Cardstock in white, ivory, taupe, pastel green, and yellow

Parchment paper

Small hole punch

Toothpick

Carpenter's glue

Decoupage medium

Old book print

Scissors

Pencil

Old bottle

Striped ribbon

5 To create the flowers, first use the tooth-pick to put a dab of glue on the bent circle area of the wire. Place a pale green floret on first, and then bend down all the petals to cover the wire circle (Fig. B).

Fig. B

6 Next, layer florets (securing each to the next with a dab of glue), mixing colors (white, ivory, taupe, parchment) but always placing a white one on top, adding another dab of glue, then attaching a yellow center. Be sure to give each layer a turn so that the petals underneath can be seen.

7 To create leaves, decoupage a page of old book print to both sides of a piece of cardstock. Let dry, then cut out leaf shapes. Curl the leaves a bit by bending them over a pencil, then glue them onto the stems.

8 Tie the striped ribbon in a double bow, attach it to the bottle, and *Voila! C'est fini!*

What You Do

1 To create stems, cut 14 pieces of the green floral wire into 7-inch lengths and 14 pieces into 5½-inch lengths.

2 Use the needle-nose pliers to bend one end of each piece of wire into a small circle, then bend the circle horizontally (Fig. A).

Fig. A

3 Use the flower punch to cut a variety of florets from the white, ivory, taupe, and pastel green cardstock and the parchment paper.

4 Use the small hole punch to cut a bunch of dots from the yellow cardstock for daisy centers.

TIP: To keep these little daisies from looking messy, use a toothpick to apply the glue.

A page from my sketchbook

Flowers sitting on the Ceiling - ornaments

Pattern Tube Flowers

seed beads?

Flat clear marble centers

Side

amethyst & rose quartz beads

decoupage with paper

then cut tube into slices

Technique 2:

Paper Towel Tubes

What could be simpler than ordinary paper towel tubes? Cut into slices, they form a myriad of floral designs. Recycling never looked so pretty.

Flowers Sitting on the Ceiling

Make several of these cheerful blooms to hang in a window!
They glow gently when the sun shines through them.

WHAT YOU NEED

Paper towel tubes

Scissors

Decorative paper
(pages 23 and 25)

Decoupage medium

Sponge brush

Toothpick

White glue

Peach tissue paper

Small, curve-blade scissors

Wax paper

Floret pattern (page 23)

Cardstock in light pink, dark
pink, green, and lavender

Book print

Flower faces
(pages 23 and 25)

What You Do

Access to a color photocopier

½-inch circle punch (optional)

Clear, flat decorative marbles

Clay-sculpting tool with bulbous end

Needle and thread

Iridescent pink seed beads

26-gauge silver craft wire

Wire cutters

Needle-nose pliers

Amethyst crystal beads

Rose quartz beads

Clear quartz beads

1. Cut one paper towel tube to a 6-inch length. Color copy the decorative paper, cut it to fit around the tube, and then decoupage it to the tube.

2. Once the paper is dry, cut the tube into six ½-inch-long pieces. The tube will flatten out as you cut it; just pop the slices back into the desired petal shape. Pinch each piece to form a flower petal shape.

3. Cut out several 3 x 3-inch squares of the tissue paper. Use a toothpick to run a thin bead of glue around the top and bottom edges of each cardboard petal, and then glue the tissue flat to each side. Set aside to dry.

4. Once the glue is completely dry, use the small, curve-blade scissors to cut away the excess tissue. Then arrange the petals on a sheet of the wax paper to form a flower (Fig. A).

5. Put a dab of white glue where the petals touch to help them form a flower shape. Let dry thoroughly.

Fig. A

Cardstock Floret

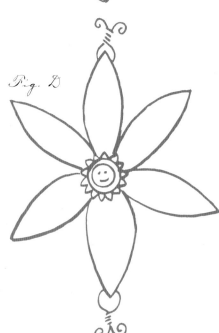

Fig. B

Fig. C

Fig. D

6 Use the floret pattern to cut two florets out of one color of the cardstock for the centers. Then cut two 1-inch circles from book print or an old handwritten letter.

7 Color copy two of the flower faces on these pages, and then cut them out with a ½-inch circle punch or scissors. Spread an even layer of white glue on the flat edge of a flat marble, and apply one flower face to the marble's bottom (picture side to flat surface so the face can be seen in the marble).

8 After rubbing the clay-sculpting tool along the edges of the cardstock floret to curl it up a bit, glue the 1-inch book print circle to the center of the floret, and then glue the flat glass marble with the face to the center of the 1-inch circle. Repeat to make another embellished floret, and then glue one to the center of each side of the flower.

Many Happy Returns

9   Use the needle and thread to string together a 2-inch length of iridescent pink seed beads. Run a layer of glue around one of the flat marbles and lay the strand of beads around the marble. Cut the end of the thread and glue it down. Repeat on the other side (Fig. B).

10   Gently poke a hole through the sides of the top and bottom petal with the needle. (Be careful not to tear the tissue—if you do, patch it with a dab of white glue (Fig. C) .)

11   Cut two 6-inch pieces of the silver craft wire. Run a wire through each hole, and then twist and curl the wires to make decorative hangers as shown (Fig. D).

12   Cut a 2-inch piece of the wire, curl one end closed, string on an amethyst bead, then a rose quartz bead, and then two small clear quartz beads. Curl the other end closed. Make two of these—one for the top and one for the bottom—and attach them to the decorative hanger.

13   Cut an 18-inch piece of wire, curl one end closed with a small loop, then string on iridescent pink seed beads to fill the entire length. Curl the other end closed, and attach it to the flower's top decorative hanger.

Smiles Valance

I purchased these baby blue wooden beads at a tag sale. When I began designing this valance, I knew I'd found the perfect use for them. It's hard to imagine anyone looking at this sunny curtain of flowers without smiling.

WHAT YOU NEED

10 paper towel tubes

Scissors

Acrylic paint in lemon yellow and pool blue

Sponge brush

Craft glue

26 1.5 mm pool blue wooden beads

52 1 mm pool blue wooden beads

Hot glue and glue gun

Polka dot paper (page 29)

Cardstock

Decoupage medium

Small, curve-blade scissors

½-inch wooden dowel, 28 inches long

Two ½-inch wooden candle cups

12½ yards yellow embroidery thread

Pencil

Embroidery needle

What You Do

1. Cut paper towel tubes into five ¾-inch slices for each flower. (I used 13 flowers for this valance.) The tubes will flatten out as you cut them; just pop the slices back into the desired petal shape.

2. Paint the slices with one coat of the yellow paint, inside and out. Let dry, and then apply a second coat.

3. Form the five petals into a floret, leaving space in the center to fit one 1.5 mm wooden bead, and use the craft glue to glue the petals together.

4. Hot glue the 1.5 mm bead into the center of the petals.

5. Color copy the polka dot paper. You'll need two 5 x 5-inch sheets per flower, plus one 5 x 5-inch piece of cardstock.

6. Decoupage the decorative sheets to both sides of the card-stock and let dry.

7. Run a bead of white glue around the entire flower on the back side and glue down to the paper-covered cardstock square. (I put a lightweight book on top to weigh it down until the glue dries. Don't worry if all surfaces don't get glued down, as long as most of them do.)

8. Use the small, curve-blade scissors to cut out around the flowers.

9. Hot glue the candle cups to the ends of the dowel, then paint the entire rod with two coats of the pool blue paint.

10. Cut the following lengths of yellow embroidery thread:

    one 16 inches (center flower will hang from here); two 22 inches (for either side of center); two 28 inches; two 34 inches; two 40 inches; two 46 inches; two 52 inches.

Be full of life and wonder.
S.E.

11 Starting at center of the rod, lightly mark 2-inch intervals with the pencil, first on one side, then on the other.

12 To attach flowers to the rod, first poke a hole in the top petal of the flower with the needle. Thread the needle with the yellow embroidery thread and—starting with the 16-inch length—fold the thread in half, tie a double knot on the end, and string on one 1 mm bead. Then go up through the inside of the flower petal and thread on a second 1 mm bead (Fig. A).

Thread on another 1 mm bead, then a 1.5 mm bead, and then another 1mm bead.

Fig. A

13 Tie this first strand to the dowel at the middle pencil mark. Follow the same procedure to attach the rest of the flowers.

14 To finish, align the three beads to form a V shape and put a dab of white glue at the bottom of the third bead to keep it from shifting.

Shooting Stars Ornaments

Imagine an all-white room with touches of silver: antique teapots, picture frames, a little silver lamp. Then imagine a few of these glittering crystalline stars hanging from the ceiling, adding just the right amount of twinkle.

WHAT YOU NEED

Paper towel tubes

Scissors

Hot glue and glue gun

Silver acrylic paint

Silver glitter glue

Needle

22- and 26-gauge craft wire

Wire cutters

Needle-nose pliers

1-inch round craft mirrors

Small clamps

Old costume jewelry

Aurora borealis rhinestones

What You Do

1 Cut the paper towel tubes into twelve ½-inch slices. The tubes will flatten out as you cut them; just pop the slices back into the desired petal shape.

2 Arrange the petals into two flower forms (Fig. A).

Fig. A

3 Cut three more ½-inch slices; cut each of these slices open at one end.

4 Open these pieces up and coil them, leaving a ½-inch tail at one end (Fig. B).

Fig. B

5 Hot glue petals together to form two flowers, then glue the three coils onto one star only (Fig. C).

6 Add several drops of hot glue to the center of the flower to help hold it together.

7 Paint both flowers silver inside and out, and let dry. Run a bead of silver glitter glue on all edges, and the front and back sides. I use four coats of glitter, making sure to let the piece dry thoroughly between each coat.

8 When both flowers are dry, layer one over the other, positioning each flower to get the doubled effect shown in the photo. Hot glue together.

9 Use a needle to poke a hole for a hanger in the top and bottom petals.

Fig. C

Fig. D

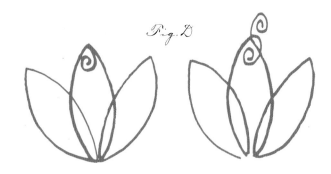

Fig. E

10 Cut a 2-inch piece of 22-gauge wire, and use the needle-nose pliers to form a small swirl on one end. Push the other end up through the hole, and then make a swirl on that end (Fig. D).

11 To make the mirror segments, cut a 2-inch piece of 26-gauge wire and make a loop at each end. Lay the wire vertically on back side of one mirror, add a dab of hot glue, and place second mirror on top of that. Apply a small clamp to squeeze the assemblage together (Fig. E).

12 Use old costume jewelry and 22-gauge wire to make simple decorative attachments. Cut about 1½ inches of wire, and make a small loop at one end. Thread on beads, attach these to the mirror segments made in the previous step, and pinch the end closed. Embellish with rhinestones for even more sparkle.

TIP: If you think you've made a mistake—like the loose ends that wouldn't stay glued down on this piece (from which it got its name!)—just go with it. These are the special surprises that make you smile later, when someone says, "How did you ever think of that?" It will be our secret.

32

Bombolina's

5½" circles

brown bags painted olive

← wire

glueball nodes & thorns

Stuff w/fiberfill

Brown Floral tape

LITTERATURE est

HELLEBORUS N°

33

Technique 3:

Paper Yo-Yos

Stitching on paper is one of the latest scrapbooking trends. I'll show you how to treat paper like cloth to make plump paper florals.

Bombolinas

These bright blossoms will add a spark of color to any tabletop or bookshelf.
Be sure to display them in a vase that's worthy of their unique beauty.

34

WHAT YOU NEED

Old merchant's cards
(page 37)

Patterns (page 35)

Scissors

Needle and thread

Polyester fiberfill

Brown paper bags

Disposable sponge brush

Acrylic paint in olive green,
auburn, and brown

Denatured alcohol

Old toothbrush

18- and 22-gauge craft wire

32-gauge cloth-covered
floral wire

Brown floral tape

Yellow cardstock

Carpenter's glue

Yellow dimensional paint

Round toothpick

Dry papier-mâché pulp

What You Do

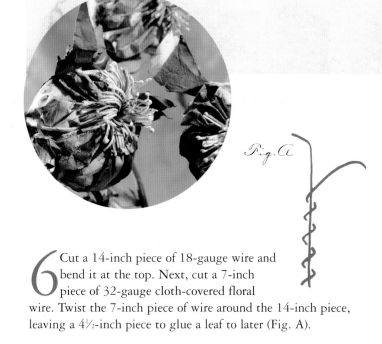

1 Color copy the old merchant cards, and cut a 5-½-inch circle out of the copy. Gently crumple up and then smooth out the paper to make it easier to work with.

2 Fold the paper over to create a ¼-inch hem all the way around. Sew a running stitch with the needle and thread. Sew all the way around, making about four ¼-inch stitches at a time. Gently gather the stitches.

3 Stuff the paper with the polyester fiberfill, then cinch it up and tie it off, leaving a ½-inch opening. Depending on how much polyester fiberfill you use, you can make the flowers appear larger or smaller.

4 Dilute the olive green acrylic paint with a bit of water, then paint a 10 x 10-inch piece of brown paper bag. While the paint is still wet, use the toothbrush to flick denatured alcohol on the bag. This will give the paper a mottled look. Let the bag dry, then repeat this procedure on the other side of the paper.

5 Use the patterns on this page to cut out the calyx and a few leaves from the paper you painted in the previous step. Gently crumple them up, then smooth them out.

Fig. A

6 Cut a 14-inch piece of 18-gauge wire and bend it at the top. Next, cut a 7-inch piece of 32-gauge cloth-covered floral wire. Twist the 7-inch piece of wire around the 14-inch piece, leaving a 4½-inch piece to glue a leaf to later (Fig. A).

7 Wrap brown floral tape around the 14-inch piece of wire, about 1 inch down from the top. Wrap the wire all the way down to the bottom.

8 To create a pistil, cut a 1 x 4-inch section out of yellow cardstock. Paint the section randomly with auburn, brown, and olive green paint. Cover both sides, then let the paint dry. With scissors, make cuts into the cardstock about ¹⁄₁₆ inch apart, stopping ³⁄₁₆ inch from the bottom edge of the cardstock. Roll up the strip and glue the end closed (Fig. B).

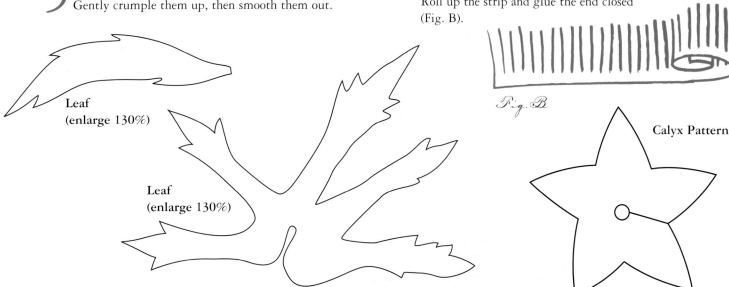

Fig. B

Leaf
(enlarge 130%)

Leaf
(enlarge 130%)

Calyx Pattern

Fig. C

9 Begin assembling the flower by gluing the rolled-up pistil onto the center of the flower (Fig. C).

10 Poke a small hole in the back of the flower. Put a bead of glue on the 1-inch bent portion of the wire stem and glue on the flower by pushing it through the hole. Glue on the calyx and the leaves.

11 Use yellow dimensional paint to make little dots on the ends of the pistils to serve as stamens.

12 To create thorns and nodes for the flower, roll bits of tissue paper and yellow glue between your fingers. Glue them randomly to the stem.

13 To make tendrils for the flower, cut four 3-inch pieces of the cloth-covered floral wire, then wind them around the toothpick. Pull the pieces off and glue them randomly to the stem.

14 To create a pod, follow the mixing instructions on the papier-mâché pulp bag. Roll the papier-mâché into a ½-inch ball. Cut a 7½-inch length of 22-gauge wire, push one end into the ball, and let it dry. Paint the pod brown, then cover the stem with brown floral tape.

15 Cut a few thin strips out of the olive green paper bag. Crumple up the strips, then smooth them out. Glue the strips to the base of the pod to form a calyx.

16 Finish by adding a few thorns and a couple of nodes (Fig. D).

Fig. D

TIP: Add some real vines to your piece for a nice effect. I used wild morning glories. Cut them green, wind them on, and let them dry in place.

Yo-Yo Mums Heirloom Wall Hanging

These pretty paper mums are a whimsical twist on the traditional fabric yo-yos grandma used to sew into a quilt. You can easily combine them into colorful rows to make a one-of-a-kind wall hanging.

What You Need

Decorative papers (page 41)

Scissors

Book print

Needle and thread

Carpenter's glue

Craft stick

Old costume pearls

Millinery velvet leaves (page 39–41)

Cardstock

Sponge brush

Decoupage medium

Clay-sculpting tool with bulbous end

18-gauge craft wire

Wire cutters

Jute twine

Embroidery thread in various colors

Embroidery needle

What You Do

1. Color copy the decorative papers at 165 percent. Cut a 4½-inch circle out of the paper. (I used 40 circles to make the piece in the photo.)

2. Cut a 2-inch circle out of the book print. (You'll need the same number as in step 1.)

3. Gently crumple up the 4½-inch circle, then smooth it out again to make the paper easier to work with.

4. Fold a ¼-inch hem all the way around the 4½-inch circle. With the needle and thread, sew a running stitch. Start by making a stitch to secure the thread, then sew all the way around the circle, making about four ¼-inch stitches at a time. Gently gather the stitches.

5. Place a 2-inch circle of book print inside the circle, cinch the circle up, then tie a knot in the thread to secure it. Leave a center opening of about ½ inch. Seal the knot with a dab of carpenter's glue. Insert the craft stick into the ½-inch opening, then gently push outward around the inner circumference of the yo-yo to make it perfectly round. Glue the costume pearls onto the circles here and there.

6. Make a color copy of the millinery velvet leaves, and decoupage the entire sheet onto the cardstock using decoupage medium. Decoupage the book print onto the back of the cardstock.

7. Cut the leaves out while the cardstock is still damp. The dampness will make it easier for you to manipulate the leaves. Mold and curl the leaves using the clay-sculpting tool, then set them aside to dry.

8. To make the hanging rod, cut a 24-inch piece of wire and twist each end of the wire into a small loop. Cut four 28-inch pieces of twine and twist the pieces loosely around the wire. The twine serves as a decorative element.

9. Cut two 6-inch lengths of twine and tie one to each end of the wire. Using these two pieces of twine, secure the 28-inch lengths of twine to the hanging rod.

10. To assemble the first vertical row of yo-yos, lay the flowers out on a flat surface and arrange them in the way you want them to appear in the wall hanging.

11 To tie the yo-yos together in a vertical row, cut 6-inch lengths of the embroidery thread. With the needle and one of the 6-inch pieces of thread, stitch through the bottom of one floret and the top of the next floret, tying the two florets together. Loosely tie off a knot in each thread as you go. Continue until you have a complete row.

12 To connect the florets in a horizontal row, stitch through the left side of one floret and the right side of the next floret, tying the two florets together. Loosely tie off a knot in each thread as you go. Continue until all of the florets are connected.

40

13 Using 8-inch lengths of the embroidery thread, one for each yo-yo, tie the top row of yo-yos to the wire. Do this by stitching through the top of each floret with the embroidery thread and tying the thread around the hanging rod. To secure each floret, make a knot in the thread and tie it off.

14 Glue on as many paper leaves as you please. Bravo! Sit back and enjoy your masterpiece!

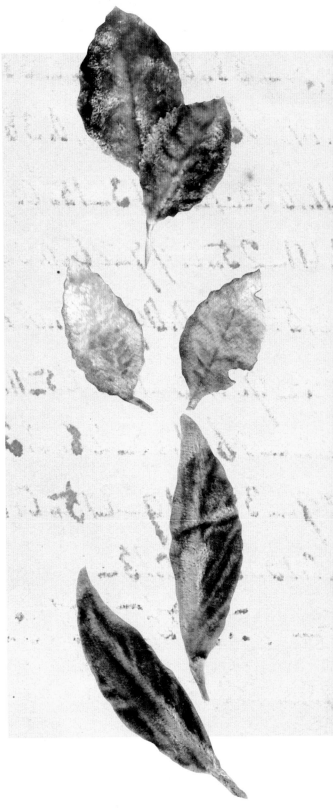

Preposterous Poppies Mini Journal

Who can resist setting down special memories in a journal as elegant as this one?
It's the perfect gift for an aspiring author or daily diarist.

What You Do

1 Glue 20 pages of the book together at a time using the decoupage medium.

2 Cut the blank paper into pieces that are the same size as the pages in the book. Glue these to the fronts and backs of the pages you glued together.

3 Decorate the front cover of your journal with an old photo or a photocopy of an old photo.

4 To make the large poppies, cut 3-inch circles out of decorative papers. Cut 2-inch circles out of decorative papers to make the smaller ones. Gently crumple up the circles and smooth them out again to make the paper easier to work with.

5 Create a small hem all the way around the circle by folding the paper over, making a stitch to secure the thread, then using the needle and thread to sew a running stitch. Sew all the way around the circle, making about four stitches at a time, then gently gather the stitches. Stuff the circle with polyester fiberfill before cinching it up and tying off the thread.

6 Use the flower punch to make the centers. I punched mine out of old business cards.

7 To make the crepe paper ball for the center, tear the crepe paper into 1-inch squares. Add a dot of glue, then roll the paper into tight little balls in the palm of your hand.

8 To assemble the poppies, glue the punch-outs to the center of each flower, then add the crepe paper balls, gluing them to the center of each flower also.

9 Tie a vintage ribbon around one side of the cover as shown in the photo. Glue the Preposterous Poppies on anywhere you like. Then, fill this very special journal with all your favorite memories!

43

TIP: This is a good place to use up all those paper scraps!

Technique 4:

Postcard Posies

Vintage postcards are easy to find in antique malls or on the Internet (or you can copy the ones I've provided). Add decoupage medium, cardstock, and a bit of floral wire, and you'll have eclectic blossoms in no time.

A page from my sketchbook

Postcard Petals in a Collar Vase

Inspired by Gibson Girl collars and vintage postcards, this playful vase-flower combination offers plenty of old-fashioned style.

WHAT YOU NEED

Cardstock

Book print

Disposable sponge brush

Decoupage medium

Scissors

Decorative papers (page 47)

Leaf pattern (page 46)

$\frac{3}{16}$- and $\frac{1}{2}$-inch hole punches

Hot glue and glue gun

Decorative-edge scissors

19-gauge craft wire

Wire cutters

Needle-nose pliers

Awl

18-gauge paper stem floral wire

12 x 12-inch sheet of decorative paper

Oatmeal or cornmeal container, 6 x 4 inches around

Old shirt collar

Three mother-of-pearl buttons

Millinery flower

What You Do

1 Use the decoupage medium to adhere the book print to one side of the cardstock.

2 Color copy page 47. Roughly cut out the decorative paper petals, and decoupage them to the other side of the cardstock. When the cardstock is dry, cut the petals out precisely.

3 Use the ½-inch hole punch to punch out one circle from a sheet of plain cardstock. Lay the circle flat, dab a bit of hot glue on top of it, and then attach the petals. You can overlap the petals a bit for a tighter, more cupped look.

Fig. A

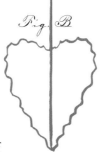

46

4 With the decorative edge scissors, cut out the Celtic Cross emblem. Decoupage the emblem to the center of the flower.

5 Cut the flower-shaped center out of the optical illusion sphere on page 47. This piece will become the calyx on the back of the flower. With the ³⁄₁₆-inch hole punch, punch out the center of the illusion sphere, then cut a slit in it down to the hole (Fig. A).

6 Cut out the black-and-white striped rectangle and the black-and-white scrolled vine element. Using the leaf pattern on this page, cut one leaf out of the rectangle and one out of the vine element with decorative edge scissors.

Fig. B

7 To assemble a leaf, cut a 10-inch piece of 19-gauge craft wire. Cover the blank side of one leaf with decoupage glue, then lay the wire over it. Put another leaf on top of the wire with the blank side down. The wire should be sandwiched between the two leaf pieces. While the leaves are still damp, bend and curl them as you wish. I made two leaves per flower (Fig. B).

8 To assemble a flower, poke a hole in the center of a floret with an awl. Cut a 13-inch piece of paper stem floral wire, make a small horizontal bend at the tip, and thread it through the hole in the flower (Fig. C). Push the flower all the way up to the bend. Secure the stem wire by dabbing hot glue around it on both the front and back of the flower.

9 Glue the calyx to the back of the flower with decoupage glue. The calyx will cover the joint. Shape the end of the leaf wire into a curlicue and wrap the leaf around the stem.

10 To finish the flower, cut a 2½-inch piece of 18-gauge floral wire, coil it up tightly, and attach it to the center of the flower with hot glue. Repeat the steps to make about a dozen of these flowers.

11 To make the collar vase, using the oatmeal container as a pattern, cut a circle out of book print and decoupage it to the top of the lid of the container. Glue the lid onto the container. Decoupage the 12 x 12-inch sheet of decorative paper to the container, and trim the paper so that it fits evenly around the container. With the awl, poke holes into the container to hold the flowers. Make one hole per flower.

12 Cut a white collar off of a shirt and glue it around the top of the vase. With hot glue, attach three mother-of-pearl buttons to the front of the vase. Glue an old millinery flower to the center of the collar.

Leaf

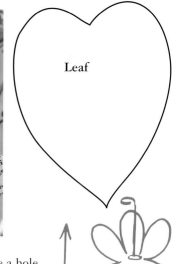

Fig. C

Metropolitan Myrtle

Entwined around a cherub candlestick, this parchment vine glints with sparkling rhinestone buttons.

WHAT YOU NEED

Decorative papers
(pages 50 and 51)

Cardstock

Decoupage medium

Scissors

Clay-sculpting tool with
bulbous end

Flower patterns (page 50)

Black-and-white text
(page 51)

Carpenter's glue

$3/16$- and $1/4$-inch hole punches

Calyx pattern (page 50)

Brown paper bag

Dusty blue acrylic paint

Disposable sponge brush

Round toothpick

18- and 32-gauge
cloth-covered floral wire

Wire cutters

Hot glue and glue gun

Leaf pattern (page 50)

Black costume pearls

Old rhinestone buttons

Needle-nose pliers

What You Do

1 Color copy the cityscape postcards and make a few copies of the chancellor label. To create the flowers, decoupage the cityscape postcards onto one side of the cardstock and as many chancellor labels as needed to fit onto the other side. The postcards will serve as the front of the flowers, and the label will serve as the back. When the cardstock is dry, lay the large flower pattern on top of it and cut out several flowers. Using the clay-sculpting tool, gently curl and mold the edges of the flower.

2 Using the small flower pattern as a guide, cut several florets out of the black-and-white text, and glue them to the center of the flower.

3 With the ¼-inch hole punch, make decorative dots for the centers of the flowers using leftover scraps of the decorative paper.

4 To make the calyx, paint both sides of a brown paper bag with dusty blue paint, and let the bag dry. Using the calyx pattern as a guide, cut several of them out of the bag. Make a hole in the center of each calyx with the ¾₆-inch hole punch and then cut the calyx open on one side. Curl the points up using a toothpick (Fig. A).

Fig. A

Fig. B

5 To assemble the flowers, cut an 8-inch length of 18-gauge cloth-covered

floral wire. With the needle-nose pliers, shape both ends of the wire into curlicues, then bend the top curl horizontally. With the hot-glue gun, attach the flower to the horizontal curl (Fig. B).

6 To cover the joint, attach the calyx using the glue gun, over-lapping it a bit to form a slight cup (Fig. C).

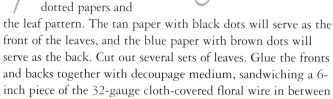

Fig. C

7 To make the leaves, color copy the dotted papers and the leaf pattern. The tan paper with black dots will serve as the front of the leaves, and the blue paper with brown dots will serve as the back. Cut out several sets of leaves. Glue the fronts and backs together with decoupage medium, sandwiching a 6-inch piece of the 32-gauge cloth-covered floral wire in between each set. Twist the end of each piece of wire into a curlicue.

8 To make the black pearl embellishments, use 6-inch pieces of 32-gauge cloth-covered floral wire. Glue pearls to both ends of the wire, then curl the wire around the toothpick.

9 To make rhinestone button embellishments, use 6-inch pieces of 32-gauge cloth-covered floral wire. Twist a rhinestone button onto one end and make a small curlicue on the other end. Curl the wire around the toothpick.

10 To assemble the vine, twist two 18-inch lengths of 18-gauge cloth-covered floral wire together. Make curlicues on both ends (Fig. D).

11 Twist the flowers and the leaves onto the vine all the way down the length of it, then embellish it with the black pearls and rhinestones. Decorate your favorite candlestick with your marvelous new creation!

Fig. D

Flowers

Leaf

Calyx

TIP: To make flowers, petals, and leaves hold their curled-up edges, use the clay-sculpting tool on them while the decoupage medium is still damp.

27 BORDEAUX. — *Rue et Porte Dijeaux. — Street and Dijeaux Gate.* — LL.

CHANCELLOR

MADE BY AMERICAN CIGAR COMPANY

"At Yule Tide"
Ye Spirit of
Holiday Fun doth
— prevail —
Come hither
and bring Thy
— Fellows" —
ons Ye Under
—Their Friends
selves — nor does
er fail To find

51

Primrose Scrapbook Cover

This delightful design can provide the perfect finishing touch for a book of pressed flowers. Covered with colorful petals, it'll inspire you to start picking and preserving your favorite blossoms.

WHAT YOU NEED

Scrapbook

Disposable sponge brush

Decoupage medium

Pink script paper
(see tip box, page 55)

Carpenter's glue

Cotton ribbon

Floral postcards
(page 53 and 55)

Cardstock

Patterns (page 54)

Scissors

Scroll paper (page 54)

Clay-sculpting tool with
bulbous end

¼-inch hole punch

Hot glue and glue gun

Yellow tissue paper

Tip whimsy girl (page 55)

What You Do

1   Use the decoupage medium to adhere the pink script paper to the cover of your scrapbook (to make pink script paper refer to the tip box on page 55).

2   With carpenter's glue, attach a strip of cotton ribbon to the left side of scrapbook cover.

3   Color copy and enlarge the floral postcards by 30 percent, then decoupage them to the cardstock. Using the petal pattern, cut out five petals for each of the two flowers that will go on the cover. While the petals are damp, use the clay-sculpting tool to gently mold and curl them. Do this by holding a petal in the palm of your hand and firmly rubbing the edges with the tool, going all the way around the petal. Let the petals dry thoroughly.

4   Decoupage the scroll paper to the cardstock. Use the patterns to cut leaves, center cups, and swirls out of the decoupaged cardstock. Cut two center cups for each flower.

5   With the clay-sculpting tool, curl and mold the center cups and the swirls in the same fashion as the petals (Fig. A).

6   Using the ¼-inch hole punch, punch several dots out of the leftover bits of cardstock. With hot glue, attach the petals to the cover, arranging them as you like. I found it was easiest to put a dime-sized dollop of hot glue on the cover, then arrange the petals around it.

7   Glue one cup on top of the other to make the center of the flower. Add a bit more hot glue and attach the cups to the flower, in the center.

Fig. A

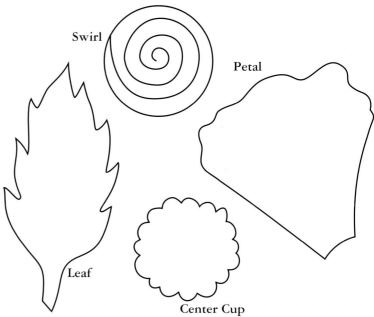

Swirl

Petal

Leaf

Center Cup

8 Tear yellow tissue paper into ¼-inch squares. Roll the tissue paper and a bit of carpenter's glue into tight little balls with your fingers. The balls should then be glued into the center cups of the flowers. I used about 10 tiny balls per flower.

9 Glue the leaves and swirls to the cover of the scrapbook. Apply glue only to the points of the leaves and swirls that lay flat against the book cover. This is meant to be a three-dimensional piece, so the flowers, leaves, and swirls should have a raised effect when you're done.

10 Color copy the Tip Whimsy Girl, then decoupage the copy to a piece of cardstock. Cut it out and mold the girl's bonnet, sleeves, and one edge of her dress. Using hot glue, attach the image of the girl to the cover of the scrapbook.

11 Finish by gluing the ¼-inch dots you made from the leftover scraps to the ribbon on the cover of the scrapbook.

55

TIP: To get the pink script background, take a handwritten letter to your local copy store and ask them to copy it on the "all pink" setting. They can also do all blue, yellow, or green!

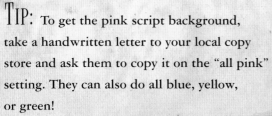

With Fond Love

Happy Memories

Best Wishes

A page from my sketchbook

Technique 5:

Cupcake Baking Cups

Normally reserved for sweet little treats, these paper cups make a wonderful craft material. Tuck a few inside each other, wire them together, and dust the edges with decorating chalks to fabricate delicate ruffled nosegays.

Decorating Chalks?

Cupcake Baking

Construction Paper Leaves

Cupcake Baking

antique silk

Lady Ashley's Barrette

Perk up an old party dress, lace throw, or pillow by clipping on this translucent baking cup barrette.

WHAT YOU NEED

Cupcake baking cups

Decorative-edge scissors

Large safety pin

22-gauge craft wire

Wire cutters

Needle-nose pliers

Decorating chalks

Wedge-shaped makeup sponge

Bleach

Old toothbrush

Green construction paper

Decoupage medium

Disposable sponge brush

Cardstock

Patterns (page 58)

Scissors

Clay-sculpting tool with bulbous end

Colored pencils

Hot glue and glue gun

3 yards ribbon, ¼ inch wide

Barrette

3 Use the decorating chalks and the wedge-shaped makeup sponge to add extra color to the edges of the paper carnations.

4 Make a mixture that's half bleach and half water. With the toothbrush, flick the mixture onto the sheet of green construction paper. Let the paper dry, then decoupage it to the cardstock. Using the patterns below, trace the leaves and calyx onto the paper, then cut the pieces out. While the paper is damp, mold the leaves and the calyx into the desired shape using the clay-sculpting tool. Rub the tool firmly along the edges of each piece until they curl up.

5 Rub olive green decorating chalk along the edges of the leaves to add shading, then draw a few veins on the leaves with the brown colored pencil.

6 Hot glue the leaves and the calyx to the flower, leaving the wire stems exposed, then attach the flower to the barrette by wrapping the wire stems around it securely. Hot glue one end of the ribbon to the barrette, then wrap it all the way around both the barrette and the wire stems, making sure the ribbon conceals the wire. Hot glue the end of the ribbon to secure it.

7 With the leftover ribbon, make three more loops and hot glue them to the sides for extra decoration. My, aren't you clever!

What You Do

1 To make a flower, fold five of the baking cups in half and cut along the top edge of each using the decorative-edge scissors. Make a loose fist with one hand, then poke the cups one at a time into the hole formed by your index finger and thumb (Fig.A).

Fig. A

2 Push all five cups down into your hand, then pinch them together at the bottom. Poke a hole through the bottom of the cups with the safety pin, then run a 6-inch piece of the craft wire through the holes and twist the wire closed (Fig. B).

Fig. B

To make the large carnation shown in the photo above, I twisted three of these flowers together tightly.

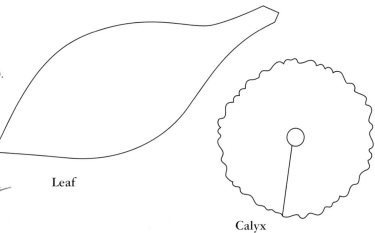

Leaf

Calyx

Eye Candy Carnation Clips-Ons

Use these colorful clip-ons to enhance a lamp or add style to a table setting. They're perfect as party favors—just write your guests' names on tags attached to the flowers, and you'll have festive keepsakes.

What You Need

Cupcake baking cups

Decorative-edge scissors

Large safety pin

22-gauge craft wire

Brown floral tape

White glue

Decorating chalks

Wedge-shaped makeup sponge

Leaves and calyx patterns (page 61)

Decoupage medium

Disposable sponge brush

Book print

Cardstock

Scissors

Clay-sculpting tool with bulbous end

Hot glue and glue gun

Wooden clothespins

Wire cutters

Sandpaper or emery board

Needle-nose pliers

What You Do

1 To make a flower, fold five baking cups in half. With the decorative-edge scissors, cut ¼-inch rings off the top of each cup and put the rings aside for later use (Fig. A). Refer to steps 1 and 2 on page 58 to finish assembling the flower.

Fig. A

2 Wrap the wire stem with brown floral tape by twisting and stretching the tape until it covers the wire completely.

3 To make the carnation fuller, fold a baking cup into quarters, cut along the top edge with decorative-edge scissors, then make several cuts diagonally, leaving a ¼-inch margin uncut at the bottom (Fig. B). Gently crumple the baking cup and glue it to the center of the flower with white glue. I used two extra cups per carnation.

Fig. B

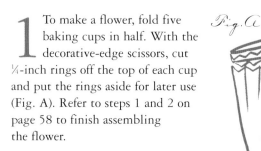

4 Use the decorating chalks and the wedge-shaped makeup sponge to add extra color to the edges of the flowers.

5 Color copy and then roughly cut out the leaves and the calyx (above and right), decoupage them to the cardstock, then decoupage the book print to the reverse side, and cut each piece out carefully. While the paper is damp, mold the leaves and the calyx into the desired shape by rubbing the clay-sculpting tool along the edges of each piece until they curl up. Hot glue the leaves to the base of the flower, then hot glue the calyx over the leaves. To create a cone shape, overlap the calyx and the leaves a bit.

6 With the wire cutters, nip off the end of the clothespin so that it's about 2½ inches long, and sand the edges smooth with the sandpaper or the emery board. Insert the flower stem through the metal spiral ring on the clothespin, then wrap it around the clothespin.

7 For extra embellishment, use the five paper rings left over from step 1. Twist the rings together so that they form a figure eight and hot glue them to the clothespin.

TIP: I use emery boards instead of sandpaper for small jobs. They're very easy to handle and work extremely well!

Bailey's Mini Carnations Wreath

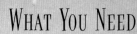

These charming mini carnations look sweet enough to eat!
Make a baker's dozen and decorate everything from a cheerful
wreath to a colorful spring basket.

WHAT YOU NEED

Cupcake baking cups

Decorative-edge scissors

22-gauge green floral wire

Wire cutters

Toothpick

Green crepe paper streamers

Leaf pattern (page 63)

Carpenter's glue

Decorating chalks

Wedge-shaped cosmetic sponge

Cotton swab

18-gauge cloth-covered floral wire

Whimsy (page 63)

Decoupage medium

Disposable brush

Cardstock

Book print

2 yards of ribbon, 1 inch wide

Glitter

Real vines

Leaf

What You Do

1 To make a carnation, fold four of the baking cups in half and cut ½ inch off the top edge of each with the decorative-edge scissors. Then make a loose fist with one hand and poke the cups one at a time into the hole formed by your index finger and thumb (Fig. A).

Fig. A

2 Push all four cups down into your hand and pinch them together at the bottom (Fig. B).

Fig. B

Then cut an 8-inch length of the green floral wire and wrap about 1 inch of the wire around the end of the floret to serve as a stem (Fig. C).

Fig. C

Use a toothpick to curl the remaining wire. I made seven of these carnations for the wreath shown in the photo.

3 Fold one of the crepe paper streamers in half vertically, then use the leaf pattern on this page to cut out three to five leaves for each carnation. Use the carpenter's glue to attach the leaves to the calyx area of the flower, making sure the wire is covered.

4 Use the decorating chalks and the cosmetic sponge to add extra color to the carnation. For an even more realistic look, use the cotton swab to dab color onto the centers of the flower.

5 To make the wreath, cut two 18-inch pieces of the 18-gauge cloth-covered floral wire, curl up the ends of both pieces of wire, and twist them together into the shape of a wreath. Then wind each carnation around the wreath as desired.

6 Photocopy the whimsy below, roughly cut it out, and decoupage it to the cardstock. Then decoupage the book print onto the reverse side of the whimsy and cut the whimsy out precisely.

7 With the ribbon, make three large bows and one small bow, then glue the large bows to the wreath and the small bow to the whimsy's head. Glue the whimsy to the wreath and add glitter dots randomly.

8 For extra texture, wrap real vines around the wreath in between the carnations.

63

Technique 6:
Crepe Paper Flowers

A popular handicraft material in the 1920s, crepe paper is enjoying a comeback, thanks to its versatility. I'll show you how to use a simple needle and thread to stitch the paper into fancy posies.

A page from my sketchbook

gather up?

print leaves

Glittering Geese

Crepe Paper glue balls

Crepe Petals

Book print curls

decorating chalks

Metal Tac

Glittering Geese Tacks and Bulletin Board

You won't be able to ignore those to-do lists when you've got a picture-perfect place like this to post them. The beautiful, blossoming tacks hold letters, bills, and memos. Organization never looked so nice!

WHAT YOU NEED

Beige crepe paper streamer

Needle and thread

Hot glue and glue gun

Decorating chalks

Wedge-shaped makeup sponge

Decoupage medium

Disposable sponge brush

Book print

Cardstock

Patterns (page 67)

Scissors

Small hole punch

Clay-sculpting tool with bulbous end

Round toothpick

Carpenter's glue

Glitter

Tacks (get the kind with a neck!)

Old frame

Corkboard

Bleached burlap

Contact adhesive

1 Begin by cutting two 36-inch strips of the beige crepe paper streamer and laying one strip evenly on top of the other. Fold the strips in half three times so that you end up with a piece that's 4½ inches long. Cut several wedges out of the crepe paper strip, leaving a ½-inch margin uncut along the top (Fig. A). *Fig. A*

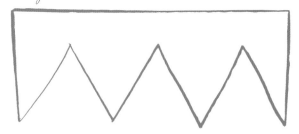

2 With the needle and thread, make a first stitch, then run the thread back through to secure a knot, and then gently sew a running stitch along the ½-inch margin, making each stitch about ¼ inch wide (Fig. B).

Fig. B

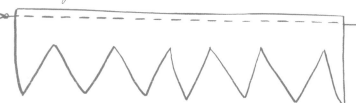

3 Gather the stitches tightly until the strip is two inches long, then make a final stitch and finish with a knot. Hot glue the ends of the strip together so that you have a closed circle (Fig. C). Use the decorating chalks and the wedge-shaped makeup sponge to add extra color to the edges of the flower.

Fig. C

4 Decoupage the book print to the front and back of the cardstock, then cut the leaves and the calyx out of the cardstock using the patterns on page 67. Add color to the leaves with the decorating chalks and sponge. While the paper is still damp, curl and mold the leaves by rubbing the clay-sculpting tool firmly along the edge of the each piece.

5 Punch a hole in the center of the calyx with the small hole punch, then cut a slit in the calyx to open it up.

6 To make curly pistil centers for the flowers, cut out a 1 x 3-inch piece of book print. Make tiny slits in the book print with scissors, then cut it into ½-inch pieces. Wrap each piece of book print around the toothpick, then slide the toothpick out (Fig. D).

Fig. D

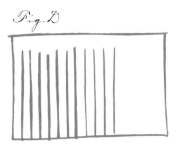

Leaf

Calyx

7 Use 2-inch pieces of the beige crepe paper and carpenter's glue to make crepe paper balls. Add a drop of glue to each piece of paper, then roll the paper into a tight little ball in the palm of your hand. Set the balls aside to dry, then add color to them with decorating chalks. Make one ball for each flower.

8 To make my Famous Glittering Dots, spread a thin layer of decoupage medium onto the cardstock, sprinkle on glitter, and let the cardstock dry. Punch dots out of the cardstock with the small hole punch.

9 Attach the leaves and the tack to the back of the flower with hot glue. Slip the calyx around the neck of the tack and secure it with the glue. Attach the pistil to the middle of the flower with hot glue, then add the crepe paper ball, hot gluing it to the inside of the center of the flower. Use a toothpick to apply carpenter's glue to the glitter dots and then add them to the flower.

10 For an easy-to-make bulletin board, pick up a fanciful old frame at a thrift store and cut the corkboard to fit inside. Hot glue burlap over the corkboard, then attach the covered corkboard to the frame with contact adhesive.

Don't worry about the future, the present is all thou hast. The future will soon be present, and the present will soon be past!

Wandering Tootsie

This gorgeous floral vine can be draped anywhere for a touch of unexpected elegance. It looks especially romantic curled around an old gold frame.

WHAT YOU NEED

White crepe paper streamer

Scissors

Needle and thread

Hot glue and glue gun

Yellow decorating chalk

Wedge-shaped
makeup sponge

Leaf and calyx patterns
(page 70)

Book print

Cardstock

Decoupage medium

Disposable sponge brush

Adhesive size

Gold leaf

Clay-sculpting tool
with bulbous end

Small hole punch

½-inch circle punch

24-gauge brass wire

Wire cutters

Amber Czech crystal beads

19-gauge craft wire

Carpenter's glue

Needle-nose pliers

What You Do

1 To begin making a flower, refer to steps 1 through 3 on page 66.

2 To make the frayed center for the flower, cut an 8-inch length of the crepe paper and fold it in half. Cut little strips into the paper, leaving an uncut margin of about ½ inch. With the needle and thread, make a stitch to secure a knot, then sew a running stitch along the margin (Fig. A).

3 Gather the stitches and cinch the strip until it's ½ inch wide. Make a final stitch in the paper and finish with a knot. Hot glue the ends together so that you have a closed circle, then use the makeup sponge and the yellow chalk to add some color.

4 Decoupage the book print to the front and back of the cardstock. Coat one side of the book print with the adhesive size. When the size is just slightly tacky, follow the manufacturer's instructions to apply the gold leaf lightly here and there to the book print.

Fig. A

5 Use the patterns on page 70 to cut the leaves and calyx out of the book print with the gold-leaf side on top. Curl and mold the leaves by rubbing the clay-sculpting tool firmly along the edge of each piece. Use the small hole punch to make a hole in the calyx.

6 Punch several circles out of the book print with the ½-inch circle punch, then punch small holes in the middle of each circle using the small hole punch. These ½-inch circles will be used later for the centers of the flowers.

7 Cut an 8-inch length of the brass wire, and thread about half of it through the hole of one of the Czech beads. Then bend the wire in half and twist the ends together (Fig. B).

Fig. B

Thread about a dozen beads this way—you'll use them as flower centers and to embellish the vine later.

8 To assemble the flower, thread one of the wire-and-bead assemblages you made in the previous step through the hole in the ½-inch book print circle, then the crepe paper center and the floret, adding a dab of carpenter's glue to each layer. Put a bit of hot glue on the back of the flower, add a couple of leaves, and thread on the calyx. Hold the piece together tightly until it's dry. I made nine flowers for my vine.

10   Cut nine 10-inch pieces of the 19-gauge wire and cover each with crepe paper in the same manner as in the previous step. Twist the brass wire stem of one flower around a wrapped 10-inch piece of wire, and then curl up each end of the wrapped wire. Use this wire to twist the flower onto the vine. Do this with all nine flowers to complete the vine.

11   Attach the Czech bead embellishments by twisting their wires around the vine as shown in the photo.

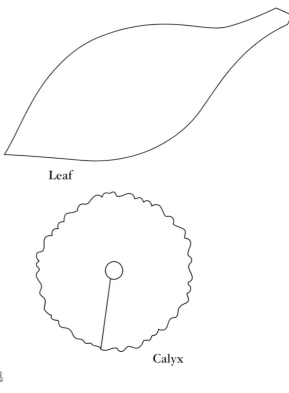

Leaf

Calyx

9   To make the vine, cut a 36-inch piece of the 19-gauge wire. Then cut several 12-inch strips of crepe paper and fold each one in half down its length. Add a dab of carpenter's glue to one end of a crepe paper strip. Fold the strip over one end of the 36-inch piece of wire, and then twist the crepe paper down and around the wire to cover it in the same way you'd apply floral tape (secure the crepe paper with dabs of glue as you wrap). When the entire length of the wire is covered with crepe paper, curl it into a pleasing form.

TIP: Always use glue sparingly. Be tidy with all types of adhesives, and it will enhance your final result. After all, you are creating a masterpiece!

Dainty Dancing Quill

It's not too late to bring back the lost art of letter writing! When you've got a pen as pretty as this one, why use email? The gorgeous purple petals will inspire you to start corresponding by hand with friends and family.

WHAT YOU NEED

Orchid crepe paper folds

Scissors

Needle and thread

Hot glue and glue gun

Crepe paper streamers in yellow and peach

Decorating chalks

Wedge-shaped makeup sponges

Lavender glitter

Carpenter's glue

Olive green tissue paper

Decorative-edge scissors

Writing pen

Two yards of variegated green ribbon, ½ inch wide

Toothpick

32-gauge cloth-covered floral wire

Green rhinestones

Package of floral stamens

What You Do

1 Cut two 36 x 3½-inch strips of orchid crepe paper, lay one strip evenly on top of the other, then follow steps 1 and 3 on page 66. The decorating chalks used in step 2 are not necessary here.

2 Repeat this same process with two 2½ x 36-inch strips and then two 1½ x 36-inch strips of the orchid crepe paper.

3 To make the frayed center for the flower, cut one 1½ x 36-inch strip of yellow crepe paper and fold it in half. Cut little slits into the paper, leaving an uncut margin of about ½ inch. Sew a running stitch along the margin and finish with a knot (Fig. A).

Fig. A

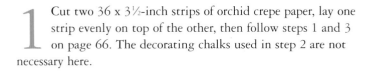

4 Cinch the stitches up tightly so that you have a little paper pompom, then hot glue the piece closed. You can add more color to the edges and tips of the pompom with the decorating chalks.

Fig. B

5 Cut a 1 x 1½-inch V-shaped piece out of the peach crepe paper (Fig. B).

6 Fold the two corners of the V into the center of the piece and secure them with glue (Fig. C).
Run a bead of carpenter's glue along the edge of the V, then dip the piece in the lavender glitter and let it dry. Make several of these pieces—you'll use them as petals for the flower later.

Fig. C

7 To make the calyx, use decorative-edge scissors to cut several 2½-inch-long strips of olive green tissue paper.

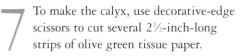

8 Wind the green ribbon around the pen begin-
ning just above the point. Add carpenter's glue
as you go, and continue winding until the pen
is completely covered. Glue the ribbon to secure at
the end (Fig. D).

9 Wrap an 18-inch piece of the cloth-covered floral wire around the toothpick. Pull the floral
wire off, wind it once around the top of the pen,
and secure it with hot glue.

10 Hot glue the calyx around the top of
the pen, then attach the 3½-inch florets, using hot glue to secure them in
place. Add the 2½-inch and 1½-inch florets next.
Tuck a few of the V-shaped petals with glitter edges
into the florets here and there, hot gluing them in place.

11 Embellish the stem with green rhinestones and
top off the flower with the frayed yellow pompom. Glue in several floral stamens. Write a long-
overdue letter to someone dear and send along the pen as a gift!

TIP: Keep plenty of wax
paper on hand. I like to
work over a surface that's
covered with wax paper—
it makes for easy clean-ups!

Fig. D

Technique 7:

Cardstock Creations

After ephemera, cardstock is the most important item on my "must have on hand" materials list. In this chapter you'll learn how to use it to strengthen and shape your creations.

A page from my sketchbook

"Midnight Blossoms" Crown

"Photo copy" real leaves

→ embellish w/freshwater pearls & crystals

gold leaf

→ shoot w/ a Pumpkin

Cardstock w/crepe paper on top

wig stand

rhinestones

Pink & Peach crepe paper

Stroke-of-Midnight Blossoms Crown

Who's got time to sit around waiting for a prince to find her?
Want to feel regal? Make your own crown.

WHAT YOU NEED

19-gauge craft wire

Wire cutters

Needle-nose pliers

Adhesive size

Disposable sponge brushes

Gold leaf

Pink and peach crepe paper streamers

Cardstock

Decoupage medium

Petal pattern (page 77)

Scissors

Round toothpick

½-inch hole punch

Wax paper

Carpenter's glue

26-gauge brass wire

Rhinestones (approximately 12)

12 real leaves (about 1 inch long)

Access to a color photocopier

Book print

Czech crystals

Freshwater pearls

Hot glue and glue gun

What You Do

1   To make the base for the crown, cut a 25-inch length of the 19-gauge craft wire. Shape it into a 5-inch-diameter circle, and twist the ends together to close.

2   The crown's decorative peaks are also formed with the craft wire. Instead of cutting a length of wire, leave the wire on the roll and unravel it as you go. Start by twisting the end around the wire circle a few times, and then form the first peak by bending the wire up 4 inches, making a small loop, bending it back down to the base, and making two or three twists to secure the peak to the base (Fig. A).

Fig. A

3   Continue this pattern all the way around the circle, making 10 peaks and leaving approximately 2-inch spaces between each peak. I used about 75 inches of wire for this. When you're done, leave about ½ inch of wire, and twist this around the circle a few times to secure the end.

4   Coat the entire crown with adhesive size. When the size is dry (it should still be tacky), follow the manufacturer's instructions to apply the gold leaf to the wire. (You may have to really press it on hard with your index finger and thumb.)

5   To make one blossom (I made a dozen for my crown), first decoupage a strip of pink crepe paper to each side of a piece of the cardstock. Once the assemblage is dry, use the petal patterns (page 77) to cut out petal shapes. You'll need five petals per flower. Curl the petals around the toothpick.

6   Use the hole punch to punch out two ¼-inch circles from the card-stock. Working on wax paper, set down one cardstock circle, put a drop of carpenter's glue on it, and add the petals one by one (unfurl each petal a bit before attaching it) (Fig. B).

Fig. B

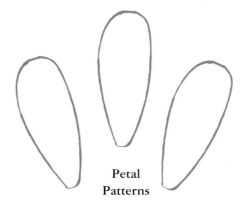

Petal
Patterns

Fig. D

7 Once the blossom has dried thoroughly, cut a 5-inch length of the brass wire and set it aside. Place the other ¼-inch cardstock circle on the wax paper, add a drop of carpenter's glue to it, then lay the strip of brass wire so it's centered on the glue and the paper circle. Put the blossom on top of this, so the brass wire is sandwiched between the two cardstock circles (Fig. C).

Fig. C

8 Let the piece dry completely. Fold the wire ends down, twist the ends closed, and curl the end as shown in the illustration.

9 Once this assemblage has dried completely, put a small dot of glue in the center of the blossom and drop in a rhinestone. Repeat steps 5 through 8 to make the desired number of flowers for your crown (make some using the pink and some using the peach crepe paper).

10 To make the leaves, first gather about a dozen real leaves that are approximately one inch long from your yard and color copy them. Decoupage the color copy of the leaves to a piece of cardstock. Decoupage the book print to the other side. Cut out the leaves while the paper is still damp, manipulate each into a curvy shape, then allow them to dry.

11 To make your crown's embellishments, cut 5-inch lengths of the 26-gauge brass wire, string on a freshwater pearl, a Czech crystal, and another pearl, and then slide the beads to the middle of the wire. Fold the wire ends down, twist the ends closed, and curl the end as shown in the illustration (Fig. D).

12 Attach the blossoms to the crown as desired by twisting their wires in place and then adding just a dab of hot glue to secure them. Hot glue a couple of leaves to each blossom.

13 Twist the bead embellishments on to attach, and off to the ball you go. Just be sure to keep an eye on the time!

Sweet happiness I gaily fling, and give you all fair warning. I'm going to dance and going to sing!

77

Sedalia's Dotted Brooch

Pinned to a vintage dress form or tucked into the band of your favorite straw hat, this saucy dotted brooch makes a unique decoration.

WHAT YOU NEED

Decorative papers and leaves (page 80)

Decoupage medium

Disposable sponge brush

Petal pattern (page 80)

Scissors

Pencil

Cardstock

Book print

1-inch circle punch

Wax paper

Hot glue and glue gun

Brooch pin back

½ x ½-inch piece of cork

Piece of old costume jewelry (I used part of a thrift store earring)

TIP: For a professional look on the brooch pin backing, decoupage a second one-inch cardstock circle with dotted paper.

What You Do

1 Color copy the dotted papers on page 80. Decoupage the black dotted paper to a sheet of the cardstock, then decoupage the blue dotted paper to the reverse side.

2 Use the petal pattern on page 80 to cut out six petals while the decoupaged paper is still damp. Curl each petal around a pencil with the black dots on the outside. Unfurl a bit, and set aside to dry thoroughly. Save the scraps of leftover decoupaged paper to use later.

3 Color copy the leaves on page 80. Decoupage the photocopy to a sheet of the cardstock, and then decoupage book print to the reverse side.

4 Cut out the leaves while the paper is still damp, and manipulate them a bit to give them some shape and life. Set aside to dry thoroughly.

5 Punch three 1-inch circles from the leftover dotted paper. Set one circle down on the wax paper, and use the hot glue to attach the flower petals, black-dotted side up.

6 Hot glue the leaves to the front of another 1-inch dotted circle. And then hot glue the brooch pin to the back of that same circle.

7 Hot glue the circle with the leaves and the brooch pin (leaf side up) to the back of the circle with the petals. Hot glue the piece of cork to the center of the circle with the petals. (This will help the piece of jewelry in the center of your petals stand out a bit.)

8 Hot glue the third circle, blue-dotted side up, to the piece of cork, and then hot glue the piece of costume jewelry to the center of the circle.

79

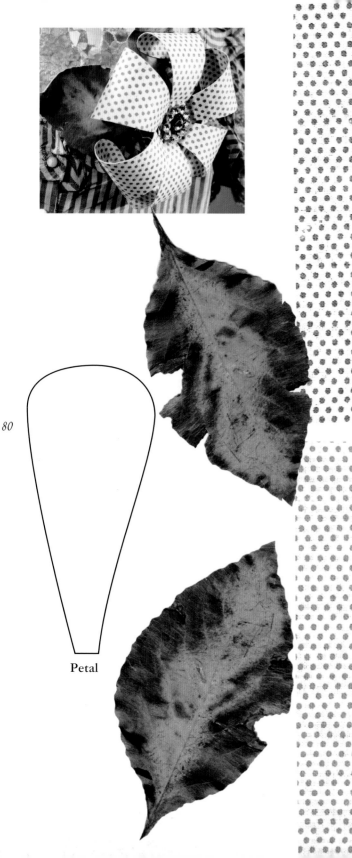

80

Petal

Consuelo's Coronet

A 1920s photograph of a lovely young lady in her wedding gown and veil inspired this playful piece. The coronet-style headpiece was in vogue during that roaring decade.

WHAT YOU NEED

18-gauge craft wire

Wire cutters

Needle-nose pliers

Polyester batting

Scissors

Carpenter's glue

Tan crepe paper streamers

Spenserian scroll paper (page 84)

Decoupage medium

Disposable sponge brush

Cardstock

Book print

Decorative leaves (page 82)

Petal patterns (page 83)

Craft knife

Pencil

½-inch circle punch

Wax paper

Masking tape

Decorative-edge scissors

Hot glue and glue gun

Costume pearls

Round toothpick

Needle and thread

Note: If you choose, you can use a store-bought hair band instead of wire as the base for your coronet.

Be sure to admire yourself!

What You Do

1 Cut a 26-inch length of the 18-gauge craft wire and bend it into an oval. Overlap the ends by ½ inch and then bind them closed with the masking tape. Next, bend the entire piece in half (Fig. A).

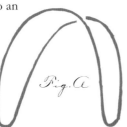

Fig. A

2 Cut the batting into a ½ x 30-inch strip, and wrap it around the wire, adding dabs of carpenter's glue as you go.

3 Fold a 30-inch-long strip of 2-inch crepe paper in half vertically, and then wrap it around the batting, using dabs of glue to secure it as you go. Cover the entire piece.

4 To make one flower, first color copy the Spenserian scroll paper. Decoupage it to one side of a piece of cardstock, then decoupage the book print to the reverse side. Use the patterns on page 83 to cut out five petals—use the large or small petals, depending on the size flower you're making. (Set aside any remaining decoupaged scroll paper; you'll use it later to make the flower centers.)

5 Cut out the centers of the petals with a craft knife, then curl each petal around a pencil.

6 Use the hole punch to cut a circle out of the cardstock. Set this circle on a piece of wax paper, and add a drop of carpenter's glue to the center of it. Unfurl the petals a bit, and attach them to the cardstock circle, one by one (Fig. B). Set this aside to dry.

Fig. B

7 To make one flower center, cut a ¼ x 8-inch strip from the decoupaged script paper for a large flower. Use a ⅛-inch x 6-inch strip for a small flower. Cut the top edge of the strip

with the decorative-edge scissors, then roll the strip tightly around the toothpick. Hot glue the tightly rolled strip to the center of a flower, then hot glue one pearl on top.

8 To make one ruffle for the base of a flower, cut an 8-inch length of crepe paper, then fold it in half vertically. Use the needle and thread to make a stitch to secure, and then make a running gather stitch across the folded edge. Gather it up, and glue the ruffle around the flower.

9 Repeat steps 4 through 10 to make as many flowers as desired. I made three large and two small flowers for my coronet.

10 Color copy the leaves on these pages. Decoupage the photocopy to a piece of cardstock, and then decoupage book print to the reverse side. Cut out the leaves while they're still damp, and manipulate them into a shape you like.

11 To begin assembling the coronet, cut several ¼ x 8-inch streamers out of the crepe paper with decorative-edge scissors. Hot glue the streamers to the sides of the coronet. Glue the small flowers on top of the streamers.

12 Hot glue the rest of the flowers on, and add in leaves as desired.

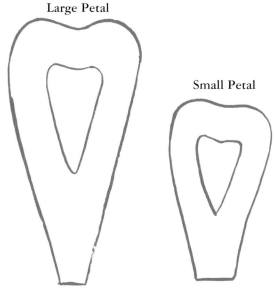

Large Petal

Small Petal

84

Flourished by Thos. E. Hill.

A page from my sketchbook

Taffies

cardstock

coat w/ wax

button centers

old rusty spring

painted orange

craft paper

Technique 8:

Waxed Blooms

Ordinary canning wax can give a lifelike texture and gentle sheen to colored cardstock blossoms. And the wax is easier to use than you might think.

Taffies

Think 1960s flower power meets CHARLIE AND THE CHOCOLATE FACTORY.
These wax-dipped flowers look sweet enough to eat!

WHAT YOU NEED

Flower, flower center, and calyx patterns (page 88)

Cardstock in orange, pink, and tan

Scissors

Clay-sculpting tool with bulbous end

Book print

1/8- and 1/4-inch hole punches

1/2-inch circle punch

Flower punch

18-gauge paper-wrapped stem wires

Wire cutters

Needle-nose pliers

Hot glue and glue gun

Two old pots (one should fit in the other) or old double boiler

Water

Canning wax

Craft stick

Decorative-edge scissors

Carpenter's glue

Old buttons

Old bedspring

Bright orange acrylic paint

Disposable sponge brush

Newsprint

What You Do

1 To make the first blossom, use the flower pattern on page 88 to cut one flower from the orange or pink cardstock. Rub the clay-sculpting tool along the edges of each petal so they curl in slightly as shown in the photos.

2 Using the pattern on page 88, cut one flower center from the book print. Use the hole, circle, and flower punches to create a variety of little dots and flower embellishments from the pink and orange cardstock and the book print. Set these aside for now.

3 Cut a 15-inch-long piece of paper stem wire. Use the needle-nose pliers to make a swirl at one end, and then bend the swirl horizontally (Fig. A).

Fig. A

4 Hot glue the flower to the bent swirl on the stem.

5 Before you melt the wax for this flower, repeat steps 1 through 4 to make more flowers from the various colors of cardstock so you'll have more ready to dip. To melt the wax, first fill the larger pot half-full with water, bring the water to a boil, and then return it to medium heat. Put the wax in the second pot, and set this on top of the larger pot. As the wax melts, stir it with the craft stick.

6 When the wax is completely melted, dip the flower in to coat it entirely. Hold the flower upside down until the wax is dry. Dip some of your flowers in wax and leave some undipped. The wax flowers will have a much deeper color than the unwaxed flowers.

7 Use the calyx pattern on page 88 and the decorative-edge scissors to cut a calyx from the tan cardstock. Use the regular scissors to cut a slit from the edge of the calyx to the center (Fig. B).

Fig. B

8 Form the calyx into a cone shape, then snip off the tip (Fig. C).

9 Wrap the calyx around the stem and hot glue it closed.

Fig. C

Flower Center

Calyx

10 Use carpenter's glue to attach the book print floret centers and the other embellishments you made in step 2.

11 Hot glue an interesting old button to the center of the flower.

12 Paint an old bedspring bright orange (or find another playful "vase"). Wrap your taffies in newsprint, arrange them as desired, and then add them to the bedspring once it's completely dry.

Have fun with your creative time!

Flower (enlarge 20%)

Waxed Licorice to Lips

Complement your décor with crisp accents of black, brown, and white. These fantasy polka dot blooms will add delightful dimension to any space.

WHAT YOU NEED

Decorative papers (page 91)

Flower pattern (page 90)

Household sponge

Decoupage medium

Two old pots
(one should fit in the other)
or old double boiler

Water

Canning wax

Craft stick

Hot glue and glue gun

19-gauge paper-wrapped
stem wire

Green floral tape

Clay-sculpting tool with bulbous end

1-inch black pompoms

White cardstock

White dimensional
fabric paint

Real leaves,
1 to 3 inches long

Needle-nose pliers

1 To make the first flower, color copy the black and tan dotted paper on page 91 directly onto the white cardstock. Then reload your copier with the same piece of cardstock to copy dots on the reverse side as well.

2 Use the flower pattern on this page to cut two florets from the dotted paper. Curl up the petals slightly by rubbing the clay-sculpting tool along all edges; the paper will wrinkle a bit, but that's the look you want. (See the tip on the next page for more on curling the petals.)

90

3 Collect several 1- to 3-inch-long leaves from your yard, and photocopy them in black and white. (You'll want to end up with enough photocopied leaves to have two or three per stem.)

4 Decoupage the copy to a sheet of white cardstock. Cut the leaves out while the paper is still damp, and manipulate them a bit to get a nice shape.

5 Cover the stem wire with floral tape by winding the tape around and stretching it while pulling it down the wire. Once the wire is completely wrapped, use the needle-nose pliers to roll a small swirl at the top of the stem. Then bend the swirl horizontally (Fig. A).

6 Hot glue one floret to the bent swirl on the stem, then glue the second floret inside that. Be sure to adjust the inside floret a quarter turn to give the flower dimension.

Fig. A

7 Before you melt the wax for this flower, repeat steps 1 through 6 to make more flowers so they're all ready to be dipped. Then follow steps 5 and 6 on page 87 to melt the wax and dip the flower.

8 Embellish the black pompoms with small dots of white fabric paint. When the pompoms have dried completely, hot glue one to the center of each flower.

9 Hot glue the leaves in place as desired, and then arrange your blooms in a playful vase.

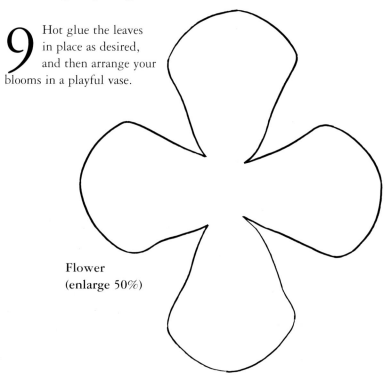

Flower
(enlarge 50%)

TIP: To help curl the edges of your petals, place a household sponge on the table, lay the flower on the sponge, and firmly press down, running the clay-sculpting tool along the edges.

Sweet Lee and Her Jardinet

As a child I enjoyed collecting butterflies, grasshoppers, and other creepy crawlers just to observe them and then set them free, thus the inspiration for this capricious vignette. (JARDINET is French for "little garden.")

WHAT YOU NEED

Florets and hat patterns (page 95)

Scissors

Cardstock in yellow, tan, and mint

⅛- and ¼-inch hole punches

½-inch circle punch

Carpenter's glue

Clay-sculpting tool with bulbous end

Decorating chalks

Brown marker

Green floral tape

Hot glue and glue gun

18-gauge paper-wrapped stem wire, about 14 inches long

Needle-nose pliers

Wire cutters

Two real leaves
(about 3 inches long)

Decoupage medium

Book print

Sweet Lee and Spider
(page 94)

Jar with lid

Awl

Rust-colored acrylic paint

Twine

Two old pots (one should fit in
the other) or old double boiler

Water

Canning wax

Craft stick

Old button

Spanish moss

Thread

What You Do

1 Use the large floret pattern on page 95 to cut two large flowers from the yellow cardstock. Use the center floret pattern on page 95 to cut one flower from the tan cardstock. Use the hat pattern on page 95 to cut one hat floret from the yellow cardstock.

2 Use the hole and circle punches to punch out a variety of sizes of dots from the mint cardstock. Then glue the dots onto all three floret pieces.

3 Curl the edges of the flower florets and the hat floret by rubbing the clay-sculpting tool along the edges. Then use the carpenter's glue to adhere all three flower florets together, one inside the other. Be sure to give each floret a quarter turn for a more dimensional effect.

4 Color the hat floret with decorating chalks and use the brown marker to add tiny polka dots.

5 Cut six pieces of floral tape, each 1½ inches long, and twist them into snake forms. These will become the calyx. Hot glue them to the top of the hat with one piece sticking up as shown in the photos.

6 Cover the stem wire with floral tape by winding the tape around and stretching it while pulling it down the wire. Once the wire is completely wrapped, use the needle-nose pliers to roll a small swirl at the top of the stem and a larger swirl at the bottom of the stem. Then bend the bottom swirl horizontally.

7 Hot glue the flower to the swirl on the top of the wire stem.

8 To make leaves, color copy two real leaves that are approximately 3 inches long. Decoupage the photocopy to a piece of cardstock, and then decoupage the book print to the reverse side. Cut out the leaves while they're still damp, and manipulate them into a shape you like. Set aside to dry completely.

9 Color copy Sweet Lee and her spider and decoupage them to a piece of cardstock. Be sure to leave a 1-inch tab at the base of Sweet Lee's feet to fold as a stand. Cut out Sweet Lee and mold her wings a bit. Cut out Spider and glue him to a 12-inch length of thread.

10 Use the awl to punch air holes in the jar lid. Then paint the lid with the rust-colored acrylic paint. When the lid is dry, tie it to the jar with the twine.

11 Hot glue the hat on Sweet Lee, and then hot glue Sweet Lee to the bottom of the jar.

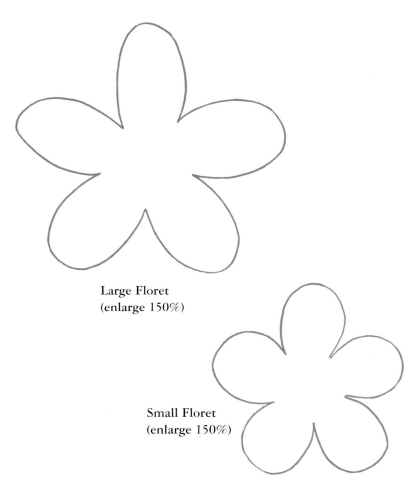

Large Floret
(enlarge 150%)

Small Floret
(enlarge 150%)

Hat

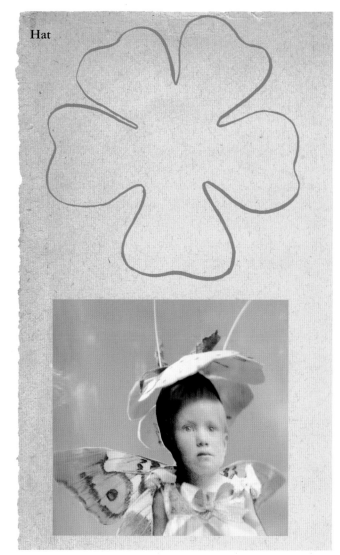

95

12 Follow steps 5 and 6 on page 87 to melt the wax and dip the flower. Once the wax is dry, hot glue an old button to the center of the flower.

13 Hot glue the flower to the bottom of the jar. Add a bit of Spanish moss. Hot glue two leaves onto the flower stem outside of the jar. Wrap the thread around the flower and let the spider dangle down!

P.S. The Spider's name is Coo.

96 *Technique 9:*

Brown Bag Roses

Lug home the groceries in them, then transform them into hearty, durable cabbage rosettes. You may never ask for plastic again!

Penelope's
...cious
...oker

— Brown Bag Ro...

Velvet band
czech crystals

...que Sera
Sera"......

pale blue

Que Sera Sera Brooch

This project lets you transform mundane brown paper bags into a gorgeous dusty blue cabbage rose.

WHAT YOU NEED

2 brown paper bags

Scissors

Dusty blue and olive green acrylic paint

Old toothbrush

Isopropyl alcohol

Petals, leaf, and curlicue patterns (page 100)

Round toothpicks

Large and small clay-sculpting tools with bulbous ends

Decorating chalks

Carpenter's glue

Wedge-shaped makeup sponges

1-inch polystyrene egg

Hot glue and glue gun

Assortment of blue and brown ribbons

Brooch pin back

Vintage costume jewelry

Cardstock

Book print

Decoupage medium

What You Do

1 Cut both paper bags into two 12 x 12-inch pieces, and paint one side of each with slightly watered-down blue acrylic paint. While the paint is still wet, use the toothbrush to flick on more water and then the isopropyl alcohol. When the two mix and dry, it creates a nice mottled effect.

2 Once the papers have dried completely, flip them over and paint the other sides using the same method.

3 Use this same technique to paint one 12 x 12-inch sheet with the olive green acrylic paint.

4 Use the rose petal patterns on page 100 to cut about 20 petals (10 top petals and 10 bottom petals) from the blue painted paper.

5 Use the patterns on page 100 to cut a few leaves and a few curlicue pieces from the green painted paper. Roll the curlicue pieces on a toothpick, unroll, and set aside (Fig. A).

Fig. A

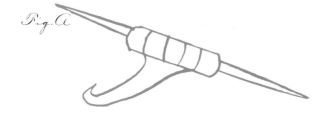

6 Use the large clay-sculpting tool to curl up the center of each petal to form a gentle cup (Fig. B).

Fig. B

7 Turn each petal over and use the small clay-sculpting tool to curl up the outer edge only (Fig. C).

Fig. C

8 To give the petals a softly aged effect, use the brown and blue decorating chalks to darken the top edges of the petals.

9 Curl up the leaves with the clay-sculpting tools, just as you did the flowers, then roll their tips on a toothpick to give them a little curl.

10 To begin assembling the rose, wrap a top petal around the poly-styrene egg, and hot glue it in place (Fig. D).

Fig. D

11 Hot glue about nine top petals around the first one as shown in the drawing (Fig. E).

Fig. E

12 Snip off the bottom ½ inch as shown in the drawing (Fig. F).

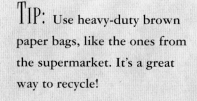

13 Hot glue about 10 bottom petals on.

14 Hot glue a couple of leaves and a couple of the curlicues to the back of the the rose.

Fig. F

15 Attach bits of vintage cos-tume jewelry to the various ribbons to make dangling decorations and attach them to the back of the rose. Then hot glue the brooch backing on.

TIP: Use heavy-duty brown paper bags, like the ones from the supermarket. It's a great way to recycle!

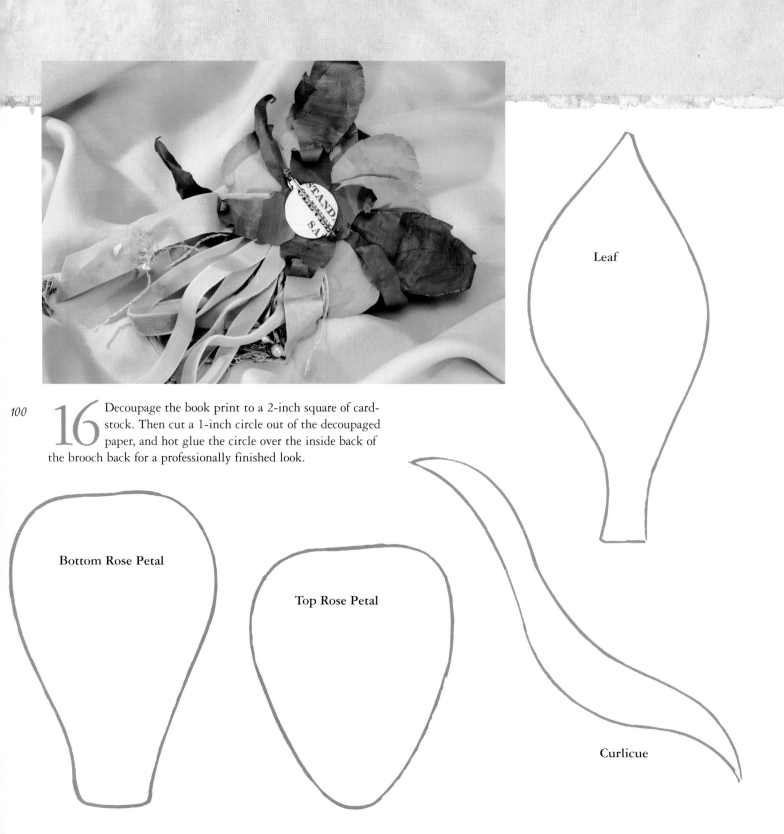

16 Decoupage the book print to a 2-inch square of cardstock. Then cut a 1-inch circle out of the decoupaged paper, and hot glue the circle over the inside back of the brooch back for a professionally finished look.

Leaf

Bottom Rose Petal

Top Rose Petal

Curlicue

Penelope's Precious Choker

I found a length of vintage brown velvet ribbon attached to a much-worn lace skirt and salvaged it to use for this choker.

WHAT YOU NEED

2 brown paper bags

Scissors

Dusty pink and olive green acrylic paint

Old toothbrush

Isopropyl alcohol

Petals, leaf, and curlicue patterns (page 100)

Round toothpick

Large and small clay-sculpting tools with bulbous ends

Decorating chalks

1-inch polystyrene egg

Hot glue and glue gun

16 inches of ribbon, 1¼ inches wide

Fabric glue

Hook-and-loop circles

Crystal beads, rhinestones, and pearls

What You Do

102

1 Follow steps 1 through 14 on pages 98 and 99 to make the rose brooch, but substitute pink acrylic paint for blue, and use brown and pink decorating chalks instead of brown and blue.

2 To make the choker, measure the ribbon to your neck, fold the ends under to create overlapping hems, and glue down with fabric glue. Attach the hook-and-loop circle closures with fabric glue. Embellish the ribbon with crystals, rhinestones, and pearls. Then attach the rose to the choker with fabric glue.

On a gray day, let it rain roses! S.E.

Jiggedy Jig Curtain Tiebacks

Add a touch of flair to your designer drapes with an extravagant curtain tieback!

What You Need

2 brown paper bags

Scissors

Acrylic paint in dusty yellow, auburn, brown, and olive green

Old toothbrush

Isopropyl alcohol

Petals, leaf, and curlicue patterns (page 106)

Round toothpick

Large and small clay-sculpting tools with bulbous ends

Decorating chalks

Yellow cardstock

Carpenter's glue

Green cloth-covered floral wire

Hot glue and glue gun

22-gauge craft wire

Wire cutters

Needle-nose pliers

Amber seed beads

2 tassels

80 inches of olive-green ribbon, 1½ inches wide

Needle and thread

Vintage beads

Assortment of vintage ribbons

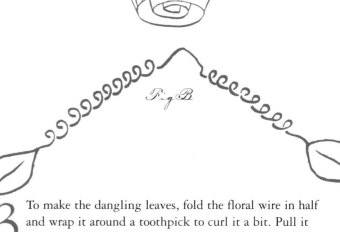

FigA

FigB

What You Do

Note: These instructions are for one curtain tieback.

1 To begin making the rose and leaves, follow steps 1 through 8 on page 98, but substitute dusty yellow paint for dusty blue in step 1, and substitute yellow decorating chalk for blue in step 8.

2 To create the pistil, cut a 1 x 8-inch strip of yellow cardstock and dab it with auburn, brown, and olive-green paint on both sides. Let dry. With scissors, make cuts into the cardstock strip about ¹⁄₁₆ inch apart, stopping ³⁄₁₆ inch from the bottom edge of the cardstock. Roll the strip up and glue the end closed (Fig. A).

3 To make the dangling leaves, fold the floral wire in half and wrap it around a toothpick to curl it a bit. Pull it off the toothpick, and hot glue a leaf on each end of the wire (Fig. B).

4 To make the seed bead embellishment, cut a 16-inch piece of the 22-gauge wire and make a small loop at one end. Thread the entire wire with seed beads, and make another small loop at the other end to close. Curl up at either end.

FigC

5 To begin assembling the rose, hot glue two petals to the pistil, one on either side (Fig. C).

Be thankful that you have the joy in you to create! S.E.

105

Fig D

6 Continue gluing petals around the pistil until the rose is as full as you like. Then hot glue a few leaves and curlicues onto the back.

7 Cut two 20-inch lengths from the olive-green ribbon (this will be the tieback foundation). Use the needle and thread to sew a running gather stitch along one edge of one piece, cinch it up, and hot glue it closed to form a ribbon rosette. Repeat with the second piece of ribbon to form a second ribbon rosette (Fig. D).

8 Cut a 1-inch circle out of cardstock. Cut another 20-inch length of ribbon, make a twist in the center, and hot glue it to the back of one ribbon rosette (this will be the tieback), then hot glue the cardstock circle to the back of the entire piece.

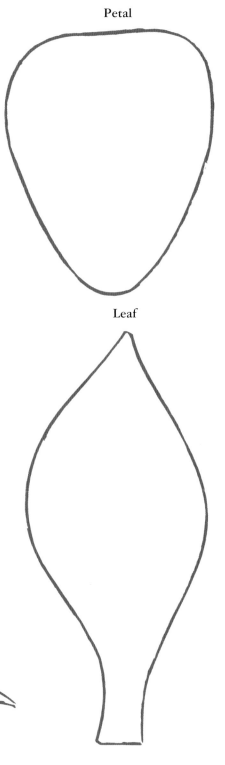

Petal

Leaf

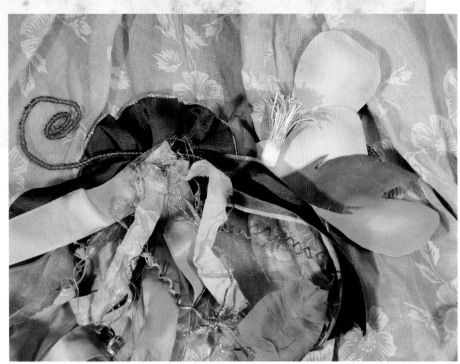

Partially completed tie-back.

9 Hot glue the tassel to the front side of the ribbon rosette. Then hot glue the seed bead embellishment and the dangling leaves to the front side of the rosette. Add a few extra ribbons and vintage beads on the wire for embellishment. (See photo above.)

10 Hot glue the second ribbon rosette on top and, finally, hot glue the yellow rose on top of that.

Curlicue

A page from my sketchbook

Crepe Paper Flowers

Split Ball

Baby Bunting's Bonnet

2 antique peach velvet baby bonnet

A WANDERING minstrel, round I stray,
To help the race as best I may,
Through summer, winter, fall, and spring,
Still "NATURE'S REMEDY" I sing.
No better age can be found
To keep the constitution sound.
It came to cure, it came to stay,

on Paper

Mache covered Pumps!

Hat Pin

Technique 10:

Crepe Paper Petals

Crepe paper is certainly one of my favorite materials to work with. It comes in a variety of colors, is easily manipulated, and holds up to time.

107

Baby Bunting's Bonnet

A sweet smiling face peeking out from a swirl of peach crepe paper makes an adorable addition to an antique bonnet.

WHAT YOU NEED

Baby whimsy face (page 109)

1-inch split wood ball (available at craft supply stores)

Pencil

Scissors

1½ inch circle backing pattern (page 110)

Decoupage medium

Disposable sponge brush

Craft stick

Crepe paper streamers in peach and green

Petal and leaf patterns (page 110)

Glue stick

Decorating chalks

Toothpicks

Cardstock

Carpenter's glue

Package of yellow pistils

Hot glue and glue gun

Brooch pin

What You Do

1 Color copy the whimsy baby face on this page. Use the split wood ball to trace a 1-inch circle around the face, cut the face out, and then cut small slits all the way around it (Fig. A).

2 Decoupage the face to the 1-inch split ball, burnishing with the craft stick.

3 Fold the peach crepe paper streamers into several layers and use the petal pattern on page 110 to cut out about 40 petals.

Fig A

the sweetest

4 Use the leaf pattern on page 110 to cut six leaves from the green crepe paper. Glue one on top of the other with the glue stick, using three pieces per leaf. Use the decorative chalks to add a bit more color to the leaf edges.

5 Roll each petal and leaf around a toothpick; leave curled up and set aside.

6 Use the circle pattern to cut two circles out of the card-stock. Unfurl the petals and use carpenter's glue to attach them to one cardstock circle, working from the outside edge into the center.

7 Glue the pistils around the center; then glue the split ball on top using carpenter's glue.

8 Glue the leaves onto the back with hot glue, and glue the second cardstock circle over that. Hot glue the brooch pin to the back. Then attach the pin to an antique bonnet.

TIP: You can purchase packages of pistils in the silk flower section of craft stores.

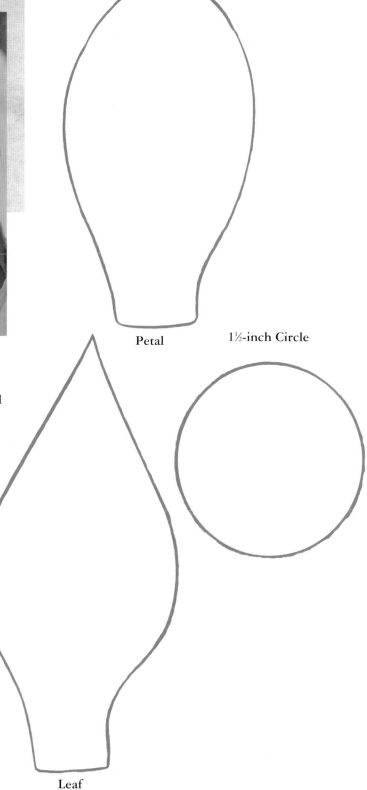

Petal

1½-inch Circle

Leaf

Love Letters Decorative Shoe Clips

The perfect gift for any shoe-lover! Create this one-of-a-kind art piece for the eclectic collector you know.

WHAT YOU NEED

Whimsy roller skate wheel circle (page 112)

Scissors

Decoupage medium

Disposable sponge brush

1-inch split wood balls (available at craft supply stores)

Craft stick

Yellow crepe paper

Petal, leaf, and circle patterns (pages 112 and 113)

Toothpicks

Olive-green tissue paper

Glue stick

32-gauge cloth-covered floral wire

Wire cutters

Carpenter's glue

Cardstock

Hot glue and glue gun

2 wooden clothespins

Vintage shoes

Handwritten love letters

Decorative scroll papers (page 114)

What You Do

1 Color copy the whimsy roller skate wheel circles below. Cut out the center circle from one circle, and then cut small slits all the way around it (Fig. A).

Fig A

2 Decoupage the circle to the 1-inch split ball, burnishing with the craft stick.

3 Fold the yellow crepe paper into several layers and use the petal pattern to cut out about 40 petals. Roll each petal around a toothpick; leave curled up and set aside.

4 Use the leaf pattern to cut nine leaves from the green tissue paper. Glue one on top of the other with the glue stick, using three pieces per leaf.

5 Cut three 8-inch lengths of cloth-covered floral wire, and wind one end of each piece around a toothpick a few times to make a coil. Glue one leaf to each coil with carpenter's glue (Fig. B).

Fig B

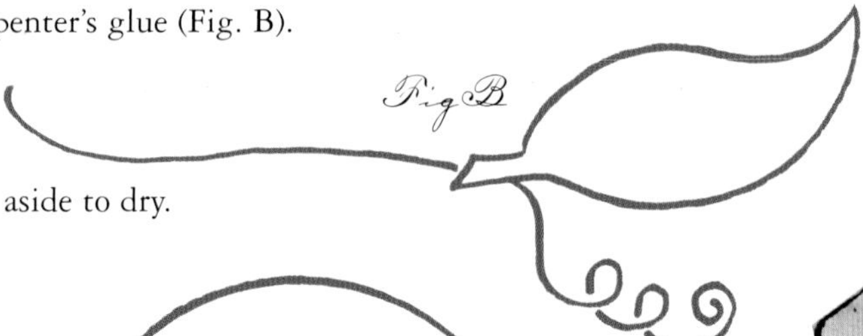

Set aside to dry.

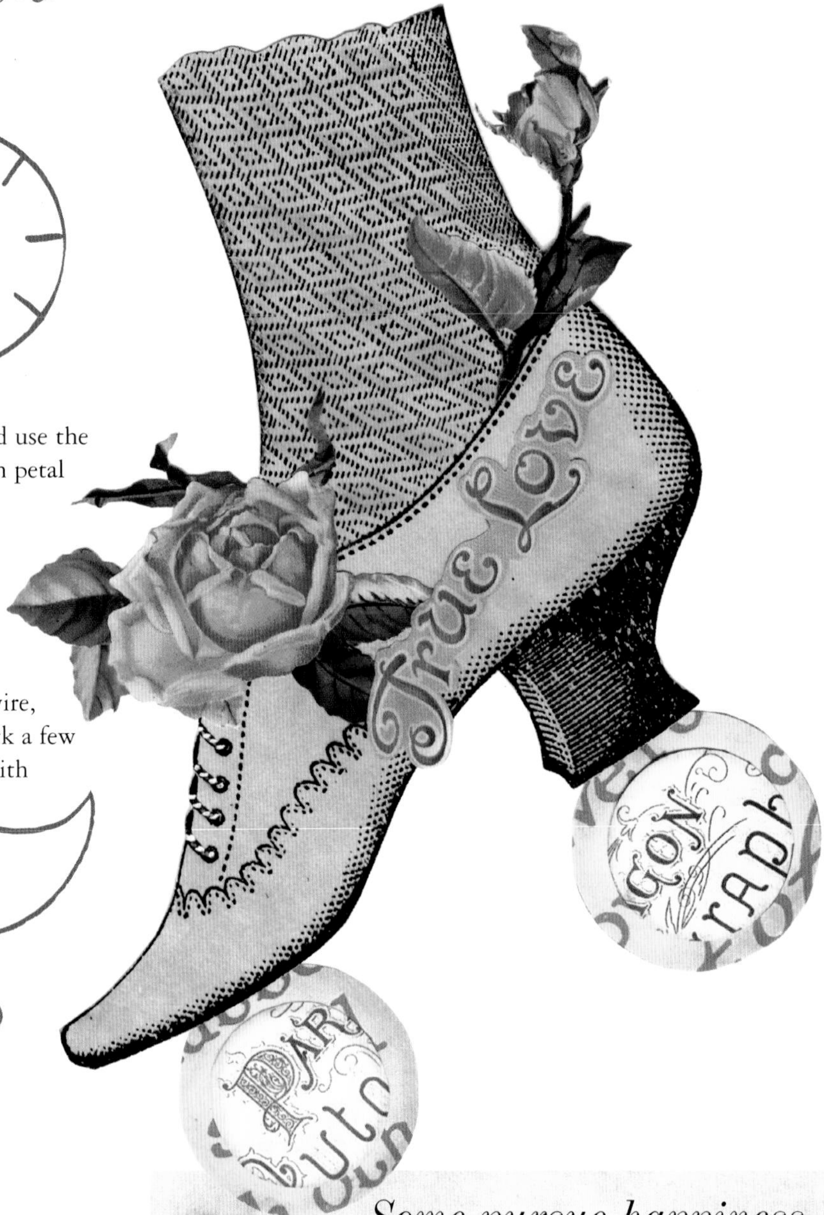

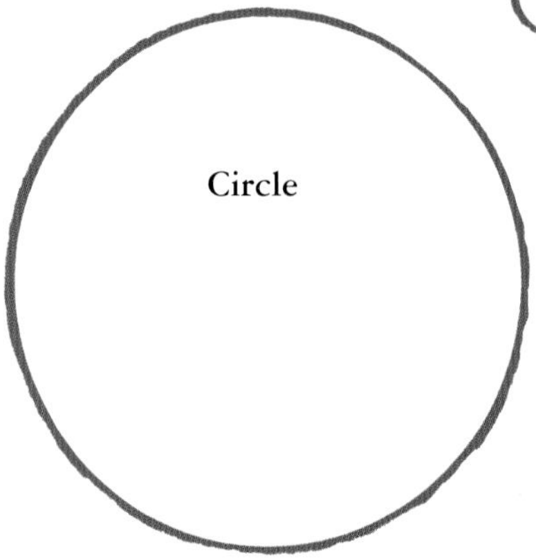

112

Circle

Some pursue happiness. Others create it!

6 Use the circle pattern to cut four 1½-inch diameter circles out of the cardstock.

7 Unfurl the petals and use carpenter's glue to attach them to one cardstock circle, working from the outside edge into the center.

8 To make the little glue ball accents surrounding the ball in the flower's center, put a drop of carpenter's glue in your palm along with a small piece of scrap paper (about a square millimeter). Roll them into a little ball and set aside to dry. Make about 40 of them. Attach these around the split ball with carpenter's glue applied with a toothpick.

9 Hot glue the leaves to the back of the flower. Then glue the second cardstock circle over that.

10 Snip ½ inch off the clothespins, and then hot glue the clothespins to back of the cardstock circle. (See photo above.)

11 To decorate the shoes, handwrite a love letter to someone special. Copy and enlarge at 200 percent. Tear into 1-inch squares, then decoupage them onto the outside of the shoes. Do the same with the decorative scroll paper, but decoupage it to the inside of the shoes.

12 Remove the shoes' soles, and use them as patterns to cut new soles out of decorative paper. Decoupage these in place.

13 Clip your new decorative crepe paper flowers onto the shoes, and then kick up your heels and go dancing!

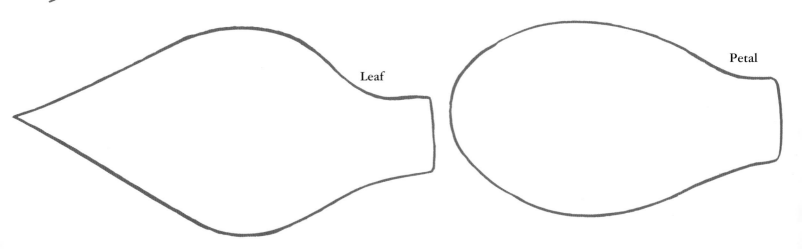

Leaf

Petal

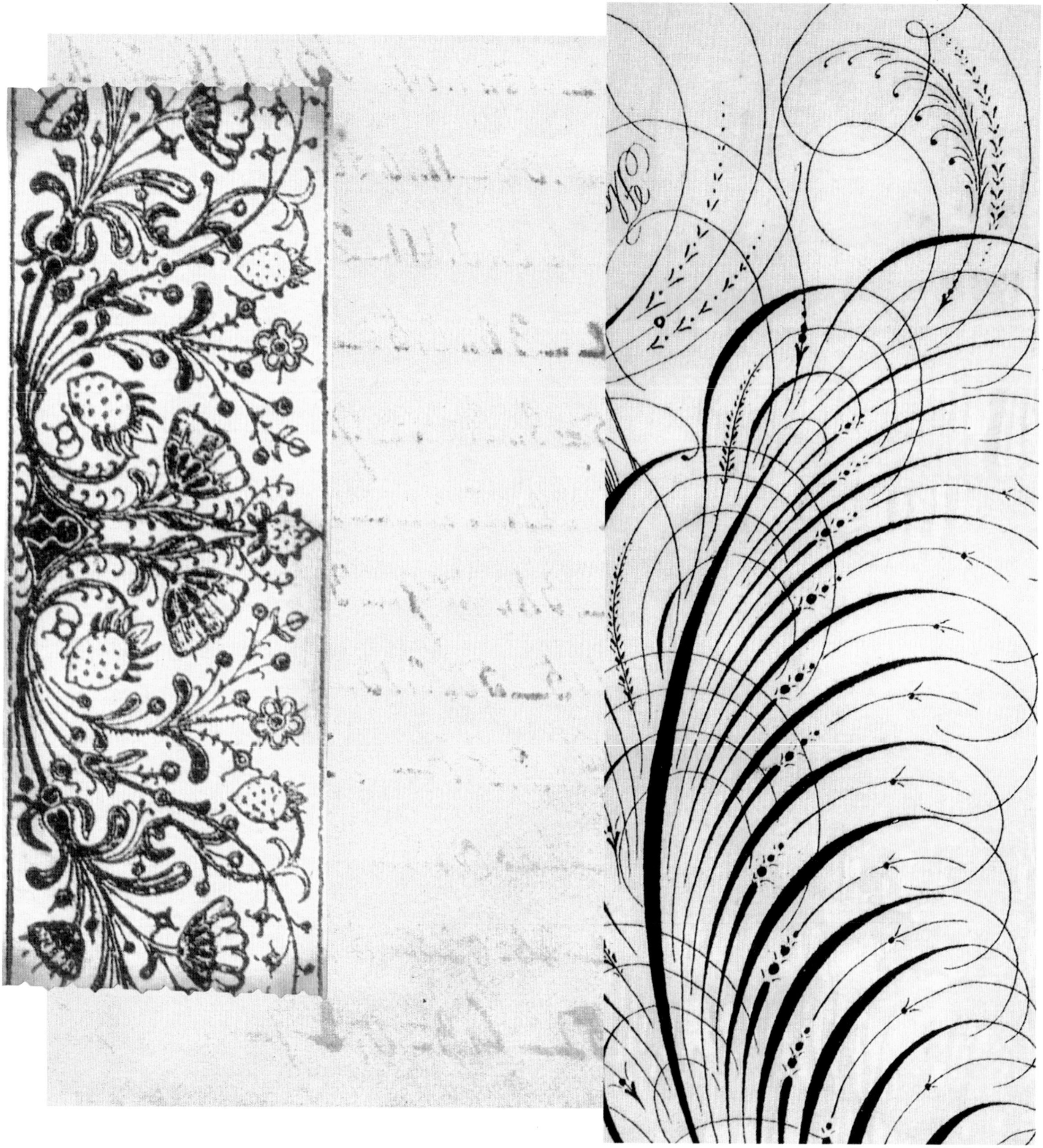

Rose Hips Hatpin

It's magic time: top hat, tails, and a dapper crimson rose. Enjoy the show.

What You Need

Whimsy circle (page 116)

Scissors

1-inch split wood ball (available at craft supply stores)

Decoupage medium

Disposable sponge brush

Craft stick

Red and green crepe paper

Petal, leaf, and circle patterns (pages 112 and 113)

Glue stick

Decorative chalks

Toothpicks

2 black pipe cleaners

2 white pipe cleaners

Carpenter's glue

Package of black pistils

Package of white pistils

Cardstock

Hot glue and glue gun

Brooch pin

Find some value in every experience.

What You Do

Fig A

1 Color copy the whimsy. Cut out the striped circle, and then cut small slits all the way around it (Fig. A).

2 Decoupage the circle to the 1-inch split ball, burnishing with the craft stick.

3 Fold the red crepe paper into several layers, and then use the petal pattern to cut out about 40 petals.

4 Use the leaf pattern to cut six leaves from the green crepe paper. Glue one on top of the other with the glue stick, using three pieces per leaf. Use the decorative chalks to add a bit more color to the leaf edges.

5 Roll each petal and leaf around a toothpick; leave curled up and set aside.

6 Twist one black and one white pipe cleaner together. Repeat to make two striped twists. Curl each one up into a swirl and set aside.

7 Use the circle pattern to cut two 1½-inch diameter circles out of the cardstock. Unfurl the petals and use carpenter's glue to attach them to one cardstock circle, working from the outside edge into the center.

8 Glue the pistils around the center, then glue the split ball on top.

9 Glue the leaves as well as the two black and white swirls onto the back of the cardstock circle with hot glue. Then glue the second cardstock circle over that. Hot glue the brooch pin to the back.

10 Pin the flower to a top hat, taking care to empty it of any magic bunnies ahead of time.

Library of Whimsies and Textures

Day by day
time's silent

wing

Added store of

Blessing bring

And every year that

hastens past

Leave you happier

than the last.

120

City and County of New York &

of April one thousand eight hundred a...

me personally came Edwin Hyde and

and on the seventh day of the same m...

me personally came Isaac Morley Jr,

to be the same persons described in and

in instrument and they severally ac...

they executed the same: and the said E...

by me privately examined apart from ...

edged to me that she executed the s...

out any fear or compulsion from him

City and County of New York ss:

of April one thousand eight hundred and

me personally came Edwin Hyde and E...

and on the seventh day of the same mon...

me personally came Isaac Morley Jr. to

to be the same persons described in and who

122

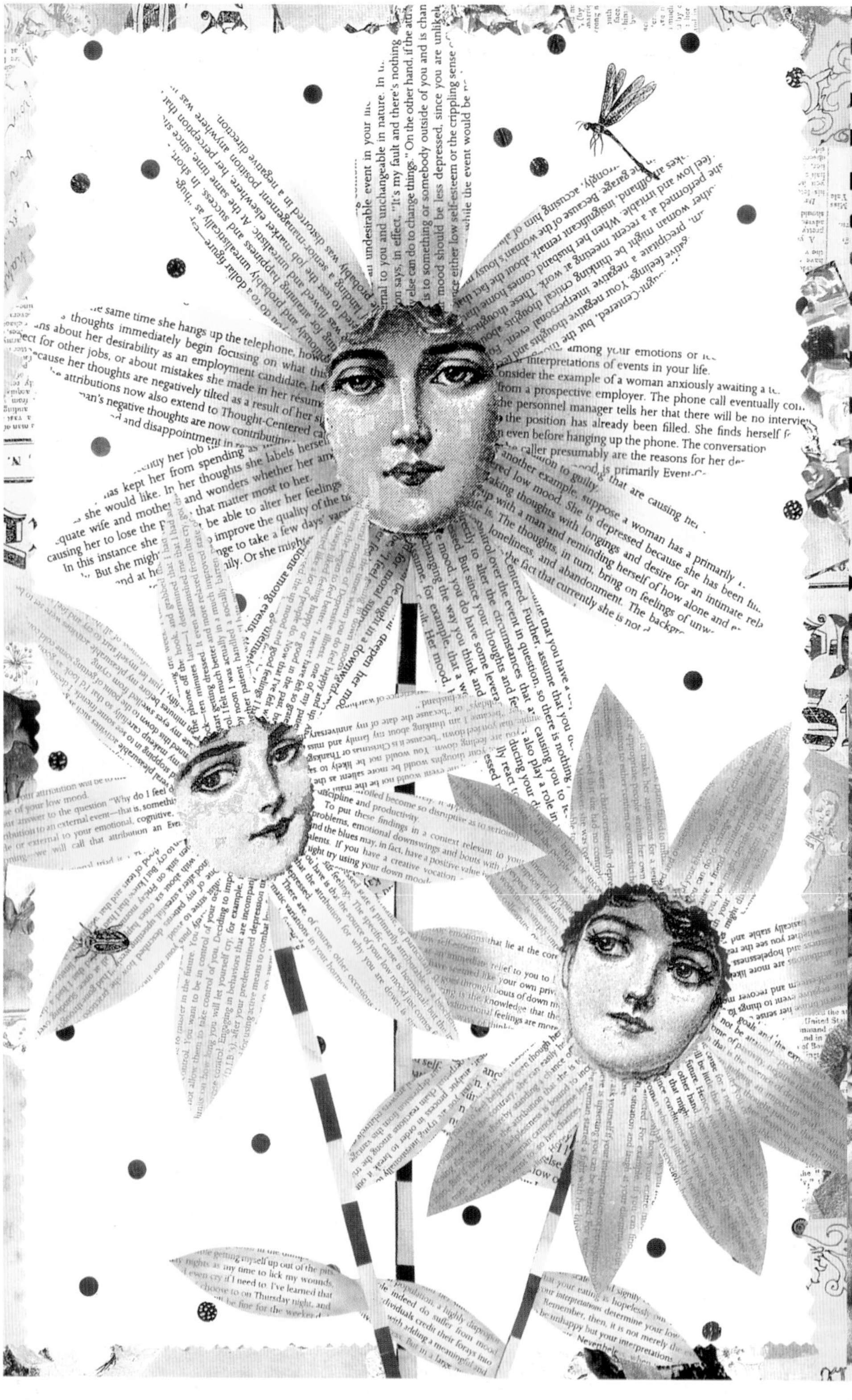

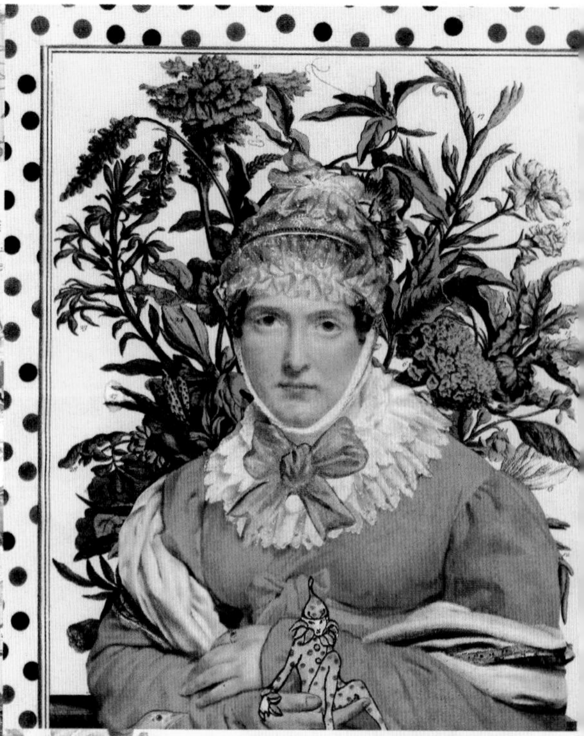

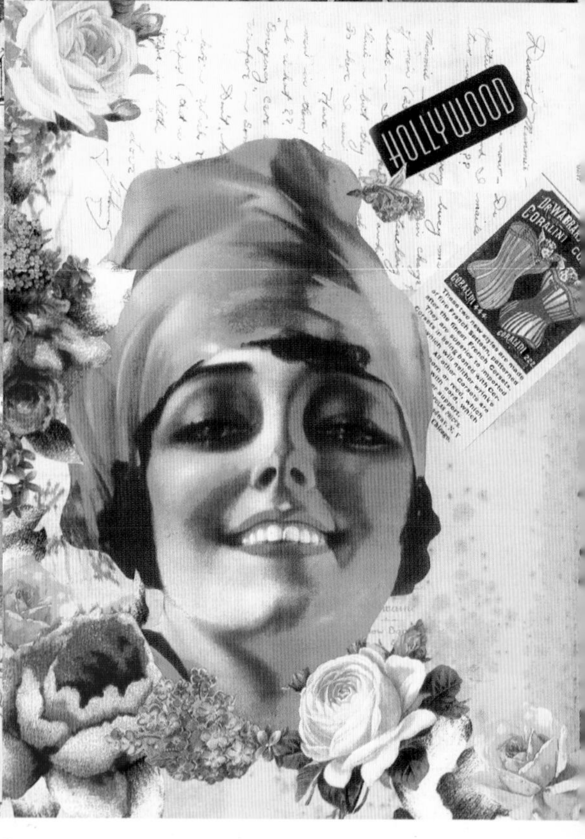
HOLLYWOOD

ABOUT THE AUTHOR

Sandra Evertson's love of crafting has
caused her to experiment in all types of
media, from papier mâché to painting to
porcelain to welding. She began making
"posh little follies" from bits and pieces of
antiques, and then moved on to designing
in paper, her favorite medium. Several
years ago, Sandra began turning her col-
lection of vintage papers into fanciful
miniature theatres, bandboxes, ornaments,
art dolls, and flowers. These original
pieces, which are all about celebrating life,
reflect her affinity for turn-of-the-century
papers, textiles, postcards, and photo-
graphs. She likes to blend humor and elegance into each of her pieces, using a style
she thinks of as sophisticated whimsy.
Sandra is the author of *Fanciful Paper
Projects* (Sterling/Chapelle, 2005) and the
owner of Paris Flea Market Designs.

ACKNOWLEDGMENTS

Thank you to: my husband, David, for all his thoughtfulness, patience, and support (my, I am a lucky girl!); my mother, Mary, for lending her talents and assistance; my family and friends for all their encouragement, especially you girls in doll class (you know who you are)!

A very special thanks to Jo, Eileen, Lauren, Paige, Kathy, Susan, and Julie for sharing my vision and just being kindred spirits in general. Thanks to Thomas McConnell for his beautiful photography and thanks to all those who worked on my book but whose names I don't know—I truly appreciate your talents. Lastly, thanks to those people in the past who had the forethought to save and preserve all the beautiful artists' works I use to create my designs, for without them my collage form of art would not even be possible. And to Romeo, you can come out from under the bed now! (In case you're wondering, Romeo is my cat.)

INDEX

METRIC CONVERSION TABLE

Inches	Centimeters	Inches	Centimeters
1/8	3 mm	12	30
1/4	6 mm	13	32.5
3/8	9 mm	14	35
1/2	1.3	15	37.5
5/8	1.6	16	40
3/4	1.9	17	42.5
7/8	2.2	18	45
1	2.5	19	47.5
1 1/4	3.1	20	50
1 1/2	3.8	21	52.5
1 3/4	4.4	22	55
2	5	23	57.5
2 1/2	6.25	24	60
3	7.5	25	62.5
3 1/2	8.8	26	65
4	10	27	67.5
4 1/2	11.3	28	70
5	12.5	29	72.5
5 1/2	13.8	30	75
6	15	31	77.5
7	17.5	32	80
8	20	33	82.5
9	22.5	34	85
10	25	35	87.5
11	27.5	36	90